If you have ever had a conversation on *The Shack*, whether with an enthusiast or a critic, you will want to invite this skilled and accessible theologian into the conversation. Before you have read a dozen pages you will know why we need to keep company with theologians. They help us keep our conversations on God intelligent, informed, and irenic.

Eugene H. Peterson

Professor Emeritus of Spiritual Theology
Regent College, Vancouver, B.C.

A scholarly specialist on Trinitarian issues engages with the explosive 'popular-level' novel *The Shack*. The outcome is a searching and helpfully revealing theological analysis, and one which is also a generous commendation of Young's contribution on Trinity and where 'tragedy confronts eternity.'

Max Turner

Professor of New Testament Studies
London School of Theology

Randal Rauser has provided a stunning exploration of William P. Young's novel *The Shack* that extends its beauty and impact, whilst simultaneously enabling discussion and reflection around some of the most awe-inspiring and essential beliefs of the Christian Faith contained within it.

Jason Clark

Founding Pastor
Sutton Vineyard, London

O's accommodation p22ff

FINDING **GOD** IN
THE
SHACK

FINDING **GOD** IN
THE
SHACK

RANDAL RAUSER

Paternoster:
thinking faith

COLORADO SPRINGS • MILTON KEYNES • HYDERABAD

Paternoster Publishing
We welcome your questions and comments.

USA   1820 Jet Stream Drive, Colorado Springs, CO 80921
         www.authenticbooks.com
UK   9 Holdom Avenue, Bletchley, Milton Keynes, Bucks, MK1 1QR
         www.authenticmedia.co.uk
India   Logos Bhavan, Medchal Road, Jeedimetla Village, Secunderabad
         500 055, A.P.

Finding God in *The Shack*
ISBN: 978-1-60657-032-6

11 10 09 / 6 5 4 3

Published in 2009 by Paternoster, a division of Authentic

A catalog record for this book is available through the Library of Congress.

Cover and interior design: projectluz.com
Editorial team: Steve Wamberg, Michaela Dodd

Printed in the United States of America

CONTENTS

To Jamie

Because Papa is especially
fond of you

ACKNOWLEDGEMENTS

In late September 2008 I delivered a seminar on *The Shack* at McKernan Baptist Church in Edmonton, AB. The conversation that ensued was animated and engaging as a number of people shared penetrating insights and deep questions relating to the content of the book. So positive was the experience that it convinced me of the need for a book to lead the many readers of *The Shack*, both fans and critics, through the nest of complex issues the book raises. At that point I shared my thoughts with Robin Parry, Consigning Editor at Authentic/Paternoster UK, and am deeply thankful for his immediate interest in the project and willingness to issue a contract based on nothing more than an informal proposal sent via email. I am equally grateful to Volney James, Publisher at Authentic/Paternoster US, who has worked tirelessly to see the book through to publication while keeping a very tight schedule. Indeed, I am indebted to the entire team at Authentic/Paternoster who have displayed professionalism and care on this project. Last but not least, I must thank my wife Rae Kyung and daughter Jamie who had to give me up for the month of October as every spare moment was spent laboring in front of a computer screen. At last I now have time to take you both out to Starbucks!

SHOULD WE LET A *THEOLOGIAN* IN THE SHACK?

I sat down to read *The Shack* after receiving a number of inquiries from pastors and seminary students who had read or heard about this publishing phenomenon. Besides selling nearly 5 million copies in less than two years, the book has been the subject of much acclaim and criticism. I was aware of the basic plot: Mackenzie Phillips receives a note in his mailbox signed "Papa" (his wife's name for God) inviting him for a meeting at the shack. The shack is the place where his youngest daughter,

1

Missy, was killed after she was abducted by a serial killer four years earlier. After accepting this invitation, Mack spends an unforgettable weekend with God through which he finds his relationship with Papa restored even as he begins healing from the great sadness of Missy's death.

Although I was aware of the book's basic premise, when I finally read the book I was struck by the boldness of the narrative as William P. Young confronted evil in all its ugliness. In a day when many Christian bookstores are full of volumes on "victorious Christian living" but few, if any, on the dark night of the soul, *The Shack* was distinctive for forcing the reader to confront a truly unthinkable crime. Even more impressive, the narrative did not stop with a safe appeal for justice for all, but instead pushed the reader on to the possibility that within God's world forgiveness could extend even to Missy's killer. This profound and daring treatment of evil was complemented by a depiction of God that was striking in its innovation and theological sophistication.

I am, and have always been, interested in reading about, discussing, and debating issues of theology. As a professor of theology and as a writer, I get this opportunity quite often. Unfortunately, theology suffers from a serious public relations problem, and this becomes evident every time I introduce myself as a theologian. Once I mention what I do, my new acquaintance typically dons a pained and slightly desperate expression as she worries about what to say next. Sadly, this describes the reaction of many Christians as well, and I'm afraid it reflects a contemporary society that too often allows busyness to crowd out reflection on the meaning of life.

The situation reminds me of the film *Jack Frost*, which tells the unlikely story of a man named Jack Frost (played by Michael Keaton) who dies in a car accident on Christmas Eve. One year later he returns to his grieving wife and son reincarnated as a snowman! Now, if you were to meet your late father reincarnated as a snowman, wouldn't you immediately interrogate him on the nature of life after death, the meaning of life, the nature of God—something along those lines? But Jack's young son Charlie is more concerned with enlisting his snowman father to beat the neighborhood bullies in a snowball fight. So preoccupied is he with trivialities that he never broaches even one profound question with his father. While we may find it hard to understand Charlie's lack of interest in his father's unusual afterlife, the fact is that there are many "Charlie Frost Christians" who are more preoccupied with the trivial equivalents of bullies and snowball fights than life's most important questions.

Why *The Shack* Is Both Story *and* Theology

When I tell people I am writing a theologian's response to *The Shack*, most have reacted with a mixture of enthusiasm and curiosity. However, one fan of the book was rather less impressed. Upon hearing of my intention, he glowered, "It's a novel, and you can't get theology out of a novel!"

I will admit that at the time that comment took the wind out of my sails. And yet, the more I reflected on his blessed honesty, the more insightful I found it to be. Here, in one terse sentence, was a succinct expression of an attitude held by many people: the suspicion that theology is simply irrelevant.

William P. Young recognizes that the best way to engage spiritual disinterest and theological skepticism is not through a lecture, but a story. And so page by page he draws us into conversation on the topics that ought to be at the center of our attention: What happens after we die? Why is there death and evil? What is the meaning of life? Who is God? And as we follow the story, we have become theologians perhaps without even knowing it.

When Mack initially receives the note from Papa he is rightly skeptical. After all, his seminary education had taught him that God does not talk directly to people anymore. If Mack had listened to his seminary professors, he would have missed out on a weekend encounter with God . . . and we would have missed out on a great novel!

Mack's theological training does not redeem itself over the next two days either. On the contrary, it consistently shows itself to be about as useful as a cocktail umbrella in a rainstorm. Mack's comment to Sarayu (the Holy Spirit) highlights the gross inadequacy of his entire theological education: "I had the right answers, sometimes, but I didn't know you. This weekend, sharing life with you has been far more illuminating than any of those answers" (Young 2007, 198; see also 91). The last thing we need is more "right answers." Rather, we need what Mack experienced: the knowledge of God. As such, it was not hard to detect in my critic's response a hint of protectiveness. After all, the last thing fans of the book need is a theologian undermining the experience of God many have encountered in this story with a lot of irrelevant and unwelcome analysis.

This critic's response to the aspirations of the theologian reminded me of a similar critique that has been occasionally launched against scientific inquiry. As the claim goes, scientists undermine the poet and philosopher's experience of the world by offering a cold and reductionist scientific analysis. Physicist Richard Feynman once offered a helpful response to this criticism. It all started when he was accosted by an artistic friend who began to wax poetically on the beauty of a flower. But then, the artist complained, when the scientist takes that same flower, he discards the experience of its poetic beauty and reduces it to a cold and dull scientific description. The complaint of that artist is common among many people who fear that science has disenchanted the world.

Feynman responded by arguing that his friend totally missed the point of science. The fact is that scientific discovery does not close the door to the beauty of the world, but rather opens new doors of beauty heretofore not even imagined!

> First of all, the beauty that [the artist] sees is available to other people and to me, too, I believe, although I might not be quite as refined aesthetically as he is; but I can appreciate the beauty of a flower. At the same time I see much more about the flower than he sees. I can imagine the cells in there, the complicated actions inside which

also have a beauty. I mean it's not just beauty at this dimension of one centimeter, there is also beauty at a smaller dimension, the inner structure. . . . All kinds of interesting questions which shows that a science knowledge only adds to the excitement and mystery and the awe of a flower. It only adds; I don't understand how it subtracts.[1]

In the same way that science, properly understood, promises to enrich our appreciation for the beauty of a flower, so I believe theology can enrich our understanding and experience of God. And that includes the experience that many have cherished while reading *The Shack*. The fact is that beneath the surface of this compelling story is an inner structure of equally compelling and beautiful theological themes. Over the next seven chapters we will journey into the labyrinth complexity of these themes and questions as we enter more profoundly into the divine mystery at the heart of *The Shack*.

---

1. Richard P. Feynman, *The Pleasure of Finding Things Out: The Best Short Works of Richard P. Feynman*, ed. Jeffrey Robbins (Cambridge, MA: Perseus Books, 1999), 2.

CHAPTER 1

WHY THIS THEOLOGIAN IS ESPECIALLY FOND OF *THE SHACK*

As a theologian, I have one big reason to be especially fond of *The Shack*. To appreciate the source of my gratitude, I need to say a few words about academic theology over the last forty years. (Trust me, this will not be as painful as it sounds!) Our story begins back in the year 1967 when Catholic theologian Karl Rahner published a little book called *The Trinity*. There, Rahner observed, "Despite their orthodox confession of the Trinity, Christians are, in their practical life, almost mere 'monotheists.' We must be willing to admit that, should the doctrine of the Trinity have to be dropped as false, the major part of religious literature could well remain virtually unchanged."[1]

By calling Christians "almost mere monotheists" Rahner meant that their beliefs about God do not differ significantly from other forms of monotheism like Judaism and Islam. But how can this be if, as Christians claim, the very foundation of their belief in God is found in the doctrine of the Trinity? Rahner's striking claim really shook up theologians as they pondered how it could be that the doctrine which is supposed to be at the heart of our faith was actually somewhere out on the periphery.

Does the Trinity Matter?

Rather than simply take Rahner's word for it, I would suggest that we test his thesis by way of a little thought experiment. Imagine that the pastor of a typical Baptist church became convinced that the Trinity was false. Instead of believing that God is three persons, he came to believe that God is one person who plays three roles: sometimes he acts as the Father, other times he acts as the Son, and yet other times as the Holy Spirit. This view is called *modalism*, and it has been considered a heresy by the Christian church since the third century.

Now if the doctrine of the Trinity really is important, we would expect that the pastor's rejection of it in favor of modalism

---

1. Karl Rahner, *The Trinity*, trans. Joseph Donceel (Tunbridge Wells: Burns and Oates, 1970), 10–11.

would send shockwaves throughout the church. But is this really what would happen? I doubt it! On the contrary, I suspect that as long as he continued to mention the Father, Son, and Spirit, it wouldn't matter if he believed they were all the same person. The church would continue on as it always had with its weekly services, Christmas pageants, potlucks, and various ministries. In contrast to this, if our Baptist pastor baptized an infant on Sunday, I bet you would have a church split by Monday! But surely this is strange: why would a peripheral question concerning the practice of baptism be more important for the church's identity than the supposedly essential doctrine of the Trinity?

Theologians knew that Rahner was right. Although we claim to be trinitarian Christians, this doctrine does not make a difference to the life of the church. But then the theologians faced the challenge of making the Trinity relevant again. They took up this challenge by doing what theologians do best: they wrote books. Lots of books. Lots and lots of books. Some were about the biblical basis of the Trinity. Others talked about the theological or philosophical dimensions of the Trinity. Still others discussed the historical development of the Trinity. And still others talked about the practical and pastoral implications of the Trinity.[2]

Many of these books were well worth reading. Indeed, some were good enough to qualify as modern classics. And yet, most were only ever read by other theologians, which meant they had

---

2. For some examples of more practically oriented and accessible treatments see Millard Erickson, *Making Sense of the Trinity: Three Crucial Questions* (Grand Rapids, MI: Baker, 2000); Robin Parry, *Worshipping Trinity* (Carlisle: Paternoster, 2005); Bruce A. Ware, *Father, Son, and Holy Spirit: Relationships, Roles, & Relevance* (Wheaton, IL: Crossway, 2005).

virtually no impact on the neighborhood church. As a result, we remain stalled in the same place we were forty years ago: few pastors know how to preach the Trinity, fewer church goers know how to pray the Trinity, and almost no one knows what it would mean to live the Trinity.

At this point you might be wondering whether the doctrine of the Trinity *ever* made a difference to the church. The answer is yes it did: the burning torch of Christian truth *has* burned much brighter in the past. To take one example, if we could hop in a time machine and travel back to the fourth century Roman Empire, we would have encountered a society that debated theology with the same vigor that Canadians today debate hockey. At that time, big questions were at stake as Christians debated a heretical view called Arianism, which said that Jesus was God's greatest creation.

The fierce public debate between orthodox Christianity and Arianism so consumed the general public that people would jump into theological debates at the slightest provocation. Strangers in the streets would get into fierce debates over various scriptural passages: for instance, how should we understand the claim that Jesus is God's "only begotten son" (John 3:16)? Did the text mean, as the Arians claimed, that Jesus was God's first creation? Or, as the orthodox Christians argued, was Jesus eternally begotten by and equal to God the Father? People of the time were *passionate* about these questions, for they recognized that the heart of Christianity was at stake.

We have a snapshot of the debate from Gregory of Nyssa, a bishop of the time. He wrote: "If in this city you ask anyone for change, he will discuss with you whether the Son is begotten or unbegotten. If you ask about the quality of bread, you will receive the answer that 'the Father is greater, the Son is less.' If you suggest that a bath is desirable, you will be told that 'there was nothing before the Son was created.'"[3] In other words, theology was to be found everywhere. It found its way into every conversation, every situation. So prevalent was theological discussion that, as Gregory's weary tone suggests, even the bishops were getting worn out by the debate!

If Christians in the past could wear out their bishops with their theological bravado, why is it that today many Christians think theology is about as exciting as watching paint dry or attending a life insurance seminar? Or to turn the question around, how can we reignite that lost passion? And how can we get average Christians excited about the doctrine of the Trinity, so that it again returns to coffee shop conversations, morning devotions, and the heart of Christian worship?

Rediscovering the Trinity in *The Shack*

While the answer to our question is surely complex, recently theology has been given a tremendous boost by, of all things, *a novel.* Not just any novel mind you, for William Paul Young's *The Shack* tells a most unlikely story! Not content simply to reintroduce the Trinity as a doctrine of mere peripheral interest, the book weaves the triune God into an engaging narrative. Along

---

3. Cited in W.H.C. Frend, *The Early Church* (Philadelphia: Fortress Press, 1982), 174–5.

the way, it goes to the heart of the most horrifying case of evil and then makes the truly bold claim that God as triune is crucial to the process by which healing is coming to this world.

First, let's say a word about the story itself. *The Shack* opens with the narrator "Willie" reporting that he has recorded everything as his close friend Mack had instructed him. (Since the name Willie is an obvious reference to author William P. Young, some readers have assumed that the book is claiming to be a factual account. But Young has made it clear that the book is fictional, albeit with a significant portion of autobiography thrown in.) We then learn that a few years prior to Willie's writing Mack took three of his children camping. At the end of a wonderful weekend, his son was in a canoeing accident, and in the melee that ensued, his youngest daughter Missy disappeared. Within hours it became clear that she had been abducted by a serial killer known as the Little Ladykiller. In a matter of hours, the FBI investigation converged on a remote shack where Missy's bloody dress was discovered, though her body was never found.

Fast-forward three and a half years and Mack continues to struggle with "the Great Sadness." Then one day he receives an invitation in his mailbox to meet Papa (his wife's name for God) at the shack. Perplexed and intrigued, Mack secretly travels to the shack on a Friday evening and is met by an African-American woman named Papa, an Asian woman named Sarayu, and a Jewish man named Jesus: all told, a rather unconventional Trinity! Over the next two days Mack communes with the three as he comes to terms with the Great Sadness and embarks on the road to healing and reconciliation.

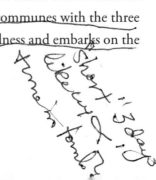

The book climaxes on Sunday morning when Papa (now in male form) takes Mack on a journey to the place where the killer buried Missy. Together they return her body to the shack for a proper burial, complete with an unforgettable memorial ceremony. After Mack shares a special communion service with Papa, Jesus, and Sarayu, he falls asleep, only to wake up in the dark, cold cabin. Mack then travels back down the mountain where he gets into a serious car accident. As he slowly recovers in the hospital the memories of the weekend gradually return, prompting the question of whether it was just a dream.

Yet when he has recovered, Mack confirms the truth of the weekend by taking Nan and the police to the grave where the Little Ladykiller had buried Missy. (Apparently Mack's experience of relocating and burying Missy's body did not really occur.) This discovery ultimately provides forensic evidence which leads to the Little Ladykiller's arrest and trial. The book ends with Mack transformed and transforming: having been reconciled with his children, wife, and abusive father, he now seeks to extend forgiveness to Missy's killer.

In the short time since its publication, *The Shack* has ignited the church's interest in the doctrine of the Trinity more than the dozens of theology books that have been published by academic theologians over the last forty years. It is wonderful (and a bit humbling) for the theologian to witness a doctrine that has long been locked in the seminary classroom now emerging as a topic of lively conversations at the local coffee shop, and all because of a novel! But while those conversations have not typically lacked for enthusiasm and conviction, many of them would benefit from some deeper background as to the theological issues at stake. It is to this end that the present book is aimed.

Six Conversations Inspired by *The Shack*

We will begin in chapter two of this book with one of the most controversial aspects of *The Shack*: the manifestation of God the Father as "Papa," a large African-American woman, and of the Holy Spirit as an Asian woman named Sarayu. This portrayal has yielded some startling, even fantastic charges (including the frenzied charge that *The Shack* promotes goddess worship!). But even if those charges are overblown, one might still wonder whether the depiction is appropriate and what it implies about our knowledge of God. In this chapter we shall explore these questions by inquiring into the way that the infinite God accommodates himself to our limited human minds, so that we can know him.

Shift to another table in the coffee shop and one might hear an impassioned discussion on how the three persons constitute the one God. On this point some critics have argued that *The Shack*'s depiction of God is seriously flawed, for it fails to distinguish the three persons. We shall enter into the center of this debate in chapter three as we explore the intriguing way that the book wrestles with the unity and distinction of the Trinity, and ultimately how it distinguishes Sarayu and Jesus in accord with their particular missions as revealed in Scripture.

Turn to another conversation and one finds a heated debate in progress concerning questions of authority and submission.

The question here concerns whether the Father is ultimately in charge of the Trinity so that the Son and Spirit eternally submit to him. Or could it be that the Father is as submitted to the Son and Spirit as they are to him? This is not a pointless question, for deciding whether there is authority and submission or mutual submission within God could have radical implications for how we organize our relationships here on earth. After all, don't we want to be more like God? The view of *The Shack* is that all the divine persons are submitted to one another and to the creation, and so all human persons should also be so submitted. We shall wade into the midst of this debate in chapter four.

While the conversations thus far are important, it is those we shall consider in the final three chapters that become for many people critical. In chapter five we will turn to ask how a God who is all-loving and all-powerful would allow the horrific murder of young Missy, a child of whom he says he is especially fond. The reason, it would seem, is that God allows Missy's death so that he can achieve some kind of greater good out of it. But what kind of "greater goods" would justify the murder of a little girl? Could it be that God allows evil for the sake of free will? And could it be that he allows evil to draw us to him while developing our moral character? Even if these answers provide a plausible general response to evil, we will feel the painful tension when we apply them to the specific death of young Missy.

Turn to another table wrestling with the problem of evil, and the life and death of Jesus Christ moves to center stage. Ultimately there is evil because creation is fallen and we are sick with sin. And so as a response, God has sent his Son to bring healing to this fallen creation. In chapter six we will consider how *The Shack* explains the atoning work of Christ, noting both what it does and does not affirm about the atonement. In particular, we will note how the book ignores (or bypasses) the language of God's wrath against sin. Indeed, in its place, it describes the Father as suffering with the Son. We will also consider the controversial question of how far Christ's atoning work extends, and specifically whether it might save some who have never heard of Christ.

As we said, the world is sick with sin and in need of the Great Physician. However, with a view of salvation as God rescuing souls for heaven, many Christians have missed the fullness of God's healing intent. And so in our final conversation we will consider the fullness of biblical salvation as extending to all creation. This vision is captured in the subtle way that the book depicts the renewal of the shack and the surrounding environs on Mack's unforgettable weekend. Evidently it is not only Mack that is being made new, but the entire creation as well.

One final word before we begin. Most people who have read or heard about *The Shack* are aware of the controversies that swirl around the book. Although I appreciate the passion of the critics, I have been saddened by a frequent lack of charity that has been shown to the book's author and its fans. And I have been especially disheartened by the advice of some influential Christian leaders not to read the book. It is true that *The Shack* asks some hard questions and occasionally takes positions with which we might well disagree. But surely the answer is not found in shielding people from the conversation, but rather in leading them through it.

After all, it is through wrestling with new ideas that one learns to deal with the nuance and complexity that characterizes an intellectually mature faith. *The Shack* will not answer all our questions, nor does it aspire to. But we can be thankful that it has started a great conversation.

CHAPTER 2

MEETING GOD
AGAIN FOR THE
FIRST TIME

While *The Shack* has garnered no shortage of praise, it has also managed to stir up its share of controversy. Undoubtedly the single most eyebrow-raising element in the book is the revelation of God the Father as "Papa," a large African-American woman who gives big hugs and swings her hips when she listens to music. Adding to the surprise is the fact that the Holy Spirit appears as a mysterious Asian woman named Sarayu. To complete this puzzling revelation, at one point Mack is interrogated by a mysterious female character named Sophia who is later described as the personification of God's wisdom (more on that later). What exactly is *The Shack* attempting to say with this startling revelation of a two-thirds female and ethnically diverse vision of God?

Some critics have been alarmed by these images, and thus have charged the book with capitulating to politically correct feminism and even promoting a pagan turn to goddess worship! Despite the gravity of these charges, other readers remain deeply attracted to the portrayal, and find the depiction of God as Mother appealing. Still others have passed over the motherly depiction of Papa and Sarayu as a relatively minor or incidental aspect of the narrative. So who exactly is correct? In my view the depiction is neither heretical nor unimportant. But it does bring us into the midst of some important and fascinating questions about the way that the transcendent God of all creation comes into our small world.

God, the Biggest Idea of Them All

At the heart of any proper understanding of God is the concept of transcendence. This word refers to the recognition that God remains far beyond (or transcends) our understanding. Consider the words of Isaiah: "This is what the LORD says: 'Heaven is my throne, and the earth is my footstool. Where is the house you will build for me? Where will my resting place be?' " (Isaiah 66:1). This verse reminds us that the God who is omnipresent (that is, present everywhere) is not limited to the buildings we erect. God as much transcends the grandest cathedral as the most humble country church. But just as we should not think our physical houses of worship contain God's fullness, so we should never think that our "conceptual houses," that is our theological understanding of who God is, could ever contain him.

We can approach the problem of God's transcendence by comparison with another big idea: the Milky Way galaxy. A little while ago my six-year-old came up and asked me the size of the Milky Way. After I explained that it is 100,000 light years across, her eyebrows furrowed as she silently pondered the answer. Then she thoughtfully replied, "Is that farther than from here to Colorado?" While I had no illusions that she would readily grasp the concept of a light year, I was caught off guard by just how far off her point of comparison was! And yet from her limited perspective it made good sense. With no conception of the distance of 100,000 light years, she was grappling with some sort of comparable scale, and so latched onto the unit of great distance most familiar to her: the two day drive our family makes every year to visit relatives in Colorado. Even so, I could see just how inadequate the comparison was! How could I possibly explain to her the enormous gulf between photons whizzing through outer space at 300,000 kilometers per second for 100,000 years, and our Hyundai puttering along the highway at one hundred kilometers an hour for two measly days?

As difficult as it may be to conceive of the vast size of the Milky Way, it is quite literally nothing when compared to the transcendent reality of God. Consider that the Milky Way, huge though it is, is only one of the more than 100 billion galaxies in the known universe. Then consider that this entire universe came to be because God uttered the phrase, "Let there be light." When

21

compared with God, thinking about the Milky Way is nothing! Theologians have tried to reflect the unique majesty of God with the concept of infinity, that is, the idea that God absolutely lacks any limit. But if God is truly infinite, then he really does transcend our conceptual houses as much as our physical ones, be they the musings of a six-year-old or the magisterial system of the greatest theologian. As Sallie McFague has put it: "The theologian must take his or her models with utmost seriousness, exploiting them for all their interpretive potential and yet, at the same time, realize *they are little more than the babble of infants.*"[1]

The God Who Accommodates Himself

You might think that with such a gulf to overcome Christians would simply lapse into silence. But on the contrary, Christians are remarkably unfazed by the uniqueness of God. For instance, if you go to church on a Sunday morning you might hear the pastor address the hushed congregation with the words: "The Lord is in this place." But what does that mean? That God is *only* in this place? Isn't he everywhere? Or one might hear the worship leader pray: "Lord, come into our presence!" *Come* here . . . as if God wasn't here already? Where is he coming from? If someone who had never heard of God before were to visit a church, he could easily think that God was a person running around the world visiting different congregations: "Okay, the Holy Spirit will be at Poughkeepsie Pentecostal Church for the 9:00 A.M.

---

1. Sallie McFague, *Metaphorical Theology: Models of God in Religious Language* (Philadelphia: Fortress Press, 1982), 131, emphasis added.

service. Jesus, you go to the Albuquerque Alliance Church for the 9:30 and we'll all meet up at St. Claire's for the 10:00 A.M. mass."

Clearly it is ridiculous to interpret such language literally. But then what lesson should we draw? Ought we to abandon that kind of language altogether? The problem with that response is that Christians did not invent this human way of talking about God; rather, it was revealed to them in Scripture. As we will note more fully below, the Bible is chock full of references to God as if he were a human person. But then if we want to understand how such language ought to be understood, we should turn back to reflect on how it functions in Scripture.

In order to understand the practice of describing God in human terms, we need to consider the concept of *accommodation*. This word comes from a Latin root that refers to the process of fitting one thing into another. To illustrate I am reminded of my days as a teenager when my bedroom was a certifiable health hazard. Occasionally my mother would build up her resolve and venture into my room with the demand that I bring some order to the disaster scene. And then with a sweep of her hand she would tell me to pick up the innumerable items scattered across the floor and put them away in the closet. Know-it-all teenager that I was, I would attempt to be the voice of reason by pointing out that it was simply *impossible* to fit all those items into that small closet. Unfazed, my mom would then quickly gather items and illustrate how, with a little folding and stacking, everything could be made to fit into the closet.

Just as my mom made it possible to fit a large amount of material into a small closet, so a good teacher knows how to fit a big idea in a small mind. Here the equivalent to folding and stacking (that is, the process of bringing the idea down to size) often occurs through the teacher's use of creative analogies and other comparisons with the student's background experience. For instance, one might explain the concept of serious illness or death to a two-year-old by invoking an analogy with a broken toy: "In the same way that your radio controlled car is broken, grandpa too is broken." But if God is infinite is even this kind of understanding possible? Undoubtedly it would not be *if* we were left to our own speculations on how the infinite God might be. Fortunately, God has spoken to us through the process of revelation and revealed a variety of points where he is comparable to our experience. Together these various points of contact anchor an imperfect but still invaluable conception of the infinite God. And even more incredibly, he does this not simply to communicate information to us (as important as this is), but to engage in relationship with us!

The Shack presents us with a rich picture of God's accommodation. Indeed, as we reflect on it, we can see that Mack's entire weekend is only possible because of God's accommodation. Since God transcends space, it is already an accommodation for Mack to have Papa and Sarayu standing in front of him as if they were human beings. Jesus' accommodation is even more radical, for his accommodation began at the incarnation two thousand years ago when the Son of God entered our space and time. With that in mind, we can see that Jesus is not simply stooping down to interact with Mack for the weekend as if he were a human person, for he *really is!* Now that is what I call *deep* accommodation! (We will return to discuss Jesus' incarnate accommodation in chapter three.)

Papa, Jesus and Sarayu also adapt themselves to Mack's limitations in other ways. When Mack sits down to dinner with the Three and begins sharing with them the joys and struggles of his family, he is suddenly struck by the absurdity of what he is doing. Mack is enough of a theologian to know that the Trinity already knows everything. So why, he wonders, should he bother with updating them on his family? When Mack poses this question, Sarayu explains, "We have limited ourselves out of respect for you. We are not bringing to mind, as it were, our knowledge of your children. As we are listening to you, it is as if this is the first time we have known about them, and we take great delight in seeing them through your eyes" (106). So even though Papa, Jesus and Sarayu already know every detail about Mack's family, they have decided not to draw on that knowledge. In this way they are able to deepen their relationship with Mack through conversation.

Any parent will be able to appreciate what Papa, Jesus and Sarayu do for Mack. Everyday when a father picks up his five-year-old from kindergarten, the first thing she wants to do is teach him all the things she learned that day. "Daddy, guess what?!" she earnestly begins from the back seat. "Did you know that bears sleep all winter? It's called hi-ber-nay-shun!" And on it goes for the entire drive home. Of course Daddy already knows that bears hibernate, and he knows most everything else she tells him too. But even so, he never brings his knowledge into the conversation, and for obvious reasons. Although she views the conversation as a way to educate her father, he views it as a chance to be close to the child he loves.

And so it is when God converses with Mack. Imagine the change in the mood of the weekend if Papa had interrupted Mack the moment he began to share about his children: "Look, Mack, we know everything. Remember? So spare us the update!" Of course God already knows, but then again from God's perspective the conversation never was about learning something new. Rather, it was about relationship with Mack.

Accommodation comes in other surprising ways, including through one's stomach! Throughout the weekend Papa, Jesus, and Sarayu share the most wonderful meals with Mack, partaking together in wonderful soups, delicious vegetables, tasty meats, and sweet baked goods. Suddenly the thought occurs to Mack: since God is spirit, God does not need to eat. So why have Papa, Jesus, and Sarayu been packing away all these unnecessary calories? Again, the point is not the food but the relationship. As Papa explains, they *ate* with Mack simply as another way to *be* with Mack: "You need to eat, so what better excuse to be together" (199). Again God is accommodating his infinite being by coming down to Mack's level and entering the human experience through the communal sharing of food.

God's Accommodation in Scripture

The lessons we learn from God's accommodation in *The Shack* provide some valuable insights when we turn to accommodation in Scripture. For the most part God does not reveal himself through direct appearances. (However, some commentators of Scripture have argued that Moses' three visitors in Genesis 18 are a revelation of the Trinity.) Rather, within Scripture God typically reveals aspects of his nature through a variety of accommodating figures of speech including analogies, similes, metaphors, and parables.

To begin with, God is often described with metaphors and analogies drawn from our experience with inanimate objects. For instance, God is described as a rock, a shield, a horn of salvation and a stronghold (2 Samuel 22:3). Some of these images are quite powerful and inspirational: think of Martin Luther's famous hymn "A Mighty Fortress is Our God." In addition, God is also compared to animals, including an eagle that cares for its young (Deuteronomy 32:11). But my favorite non-human image of God is found in Psalm 18. In this passage the psalmist is crying for deliverance from his oppressors when suddenly God appears as a fire-breathing dragon swooping down to bring deliverance! "Smoke rose from his nostrils; consuming fire came from his mouth, burning coals blazed out of it. He parted the heavens and came down; dark clouds were under his feet" (Psalm 18:8–9). In my view this just might be the coolest description of God in all Scripture!

Images of God as a fortress or protective dragon can be powerful. But the richest images are surely those that describe God as if he were a human person. As such, it is little surprise that human language provides the normative form of referring to God within church. Rather than functioning literally, this language is clearly anthropomorphic (a word that comes from the Greek words for human and form), meaning that it describes God as if he had a human form or human abilities. Consider again the notion of space. While God exists everywhere, it is very difficult to think of and relate to a God who is omnipresent. And so, Scripture accommodates God to our experience by describing him *as if* he had a physical body. Thus we find references to the finger of God (Exodus 31:18), the hand and arm of God (Deuteronomy 5:15) and the face of God (2 Chronicles 30:9). These types of descriptions are not simply more vivid or natural but can actually be quite powerful. For instance, when God condemns Israel's rebellion he declares: "I will certainly hide my face in that day" (Deuteronomy 31:18). This is a powerful way to communicate God's disapproval but it would not be available to us if we were restricted to literal speech about the omnipresent God.

Scripture also accommodates God in his infinite knowledge by often describing God as if he were limited in his understanding. Keep in mind the image of Papa, Jesus, and Sarayu withholding their perfect knowledge so that they might commune with Mack. Similarly, within Scripture God frequently withholds his knowledge. (The point is not that God becomes ignorant, but that he does not make his knowledge part of the human interaction.) For instance, just when Abraham was about to sacrifice Isaac, God intervened and said, "Now I know that you fear God" (Genesis 22:12). If we interpreted this literally then it would imply that God did not know whether Abraham would be faithful until he tested him. But that cannot be so, for all the days of Abraham's life were written in God's book before one of them came to be (Psalm 139:16). If God knows all events before they occur, including every detail of Abraham's life, then what was the point of the testing? The point was not that *God* would learn Abraham was fully committed to him, but rather that *Abraham* would learn from and be strengthened by his own faithfulness. Thus every time God is depicted as learning, Scripture is accommodating to us. The same point applies when we read of God receiving a report of the sin of Sodom and Gomorrah and resolving to go down to see whether it really is true (Genesis 18:20–21). God is surely not ignorant of the ongoing events at different geographic locations!

The case of Hezekiah provides an excellent biblical parallel for God's accommodation to Mack. After Hezekiah falls ill, God tells him that he will die. Upon hearing this shocking news, Hezekiah begins to weep before the Lord as he pleads for a longer life. In response, God sends Isaiah to tell Hezekiah that he has decided to extend the king's life (2 Kings 20:1–6). If we understood this text literally, then we would conclude that God changed his mind after hearing Hezekiah's prayers. But if God knows the future perfectly, then he cannot change his mind (Numbers 23:19). God always knew that Hezekiah would pray for a longer life. And God also knew that he would grant the request. But then it must be that when God originally said Hezekiah's death was imminent, God knew that it actually was not. So why did he originally tell Hezekiah he would die? Think back to Mack's question to Papa, Jesus, and Sarayu. Why did they act as if they did not already know every detail about Mack's family? The point was so that they might have a conversation

29

with Mack. And why did God not tell Hezekiah the ultimate outcome at the beginning? So that Hezekiah would come to God in prayer in a way that would benefit him. God stoops down to our level and interacts with us as if he were a human being, *and he does it so we can come into relationship with him.*

In addition to being revealed in human form and with human limitations, God is also revealed in specific human roles. For instance, God is described as a potter (Isaiah 64:8), a father (Deuteronomy 32:6), a warrior (Exodus 15:3), a king (Exodus 15:18), a singer (Zephaniah 3:17), a husband (Isaiah 54:5), and even as like a drunken soldier awakening from sleep (Psalm 78:65)! Since these images are all explicitly masculine or at least gender neutral, many Christians have found it natural to think of God wholly in male terms. As Mack admitted to Willie, "I've always sort of pictured him as a really big grandpa with a long white flowing beard, sort of like Gandalf in Tolkein's *Lord of the Rings*" (73). For this reason it is all the more jarring when Papa appears to Mack as a large African-American woman and the Holy Spirit as an Asian woman named Sarayu. With this shocking encounter, Mack was forced to reflect more deeply upon his thinking about God. In the next two sections we will consider why God appears to Mack as a way to challenge his dependence on a narrow range of images, and to relieve Mack's burden of having to conceive of God as Father.

When an Icon Becomes an Idol

One of my most vivid memories of a visit to Russia in 1994 was the sheer abundance of icons on sale at the street markets.

Looking at the piles of icons spread out on blankets for pass-ersby, it was hard to believe that these innocuous little wooden painted images of Christ, saints, and angels had in the past been the cause of fighting and bloodshed. Yet such was the case in the ninth century when advocates of icon use squared off against the critics. Many of the fiercest critics alleged that icons of God violated the biblical prohibition against depicting God (Exodus 20:4). Further, the critics denounced all icons as leading to idol worship. The perception was understandable given that devotees often sat prostrated before an icon in prayer, thereby creating the impression that they were worshipping a piece of wood. Yet advocates of the icons were quick to defend their use. These little painted images are not idols, they explained, but rather windows through which we can think about God.

Christians may continue to debate the use of icons. But the figurative accommodating descriptions of God that we find in Scripture could well be described as literary icons—icons that we read. Scripture certainly paints some vivid word-pictures of God. (Think again of the God-as-a-dragon image of Psalm 18!) Just as the user of painted icons must never confuse them with the reality they represent, so we should not confuse the literary icons of Scripture with literal descriptions. Instead, we should always keep in mind their function as accommodations to our limited intellects. As John Calvin put it (with a touch of impatience): "For who even of slight intelligence does not understand that, as nurses commonly do with infants, God is

31

wont in a measure to 'lisp' in speaking to us?"[2] That is, just as a nurse or mother accommodates the limitations of an infant with baby talk, so God accommodates to our limitations by describing himself within the range of human experience, often by speaking *as if* he were a human.

Certainly most Christians understand that God is not literally a king sitting on a physical throne, or a warrior clad in studded armor, or a dragon flying down from heaven! This said, if we become too attached to one or another image, we might find that the line between accommodated image and literal reality becomes blurred. This is the danger with Mack's tendency to assume that, in some sense, God just *is* a Gandalf grandfather. And so when Mack arrives at the cabin he receives the jarring reminder that God is much more than any image: "Two women and a man and none of them white? Then again, why had he naturally assumed that God would be white?" (87).

Why indeed? Perhaps because it is very natural to allow the limited range of divine accommodations with which we are most comfortable to become rigid, and eventually exclusive. (In the same way, if we come to church week after week and sit in the same spot in the same pew, we might come to think that is *our* spot. This assumption can lead to great consternation when we come one week and *find some unwelcome stranger sitting in our spot!*) When God shows up in this "unorthodox" form, Mack begins to realize how narrow his understanding of God had been: "all his visuals for God were very white and very male" (93).

---

2. John Calvin, *Institutes of the Christian Religion*, vol. 1, ed. John T. McNeill, trans. Ford Lewis Battles (London: SCM Press, 1961), 121.

The point is not that Mack should *stop* thinking of God as a Gandalf grandfather, but rather that he needs to expand beyond this limiting picture of God simply as a stately white male. As Papa explains:

> Mackenzie, I am neither male nor female, even though both genders are derived from my nature. If I choose to *appear* to you as a man or a woman, it's because I love you. For me to appear as a woman and suggest that you call me Papa is simply to mix metaphors, to help you keep from falling so easily back into your religious conditioning. (93)

So God appears as an African-American woman to remind Mack that God is much greater than any literary icons in Scripture. Whatever you can say about God, whichever image you use to think of him, he always exists beyond these conceptions. It is a lesson that Mack will not soon forget.

God Meets You Where You Are

Successful accommodators recognize that "one size does not fit all." Rather, an effective teacher will choose the right accommodation for an audience's experience and knowledge.

Consider the way that Jesus sought to communicate a really big and abstract idea: the growth of the Kingdom of God. Given his Jewish Palestinian audience, he lighted upon something familiar to their context: the way a tiny mustard seed grows into a verdant plant in which birds may nest. There is no doubt that this was a great image for someone living in Judea. But what about those of us who have never seen a mustard seed or plant? While we might understand the point of the parable, it would be that much more powerful if it was explained with a more familiar image. Now consider Eugene Peterson's translation of this parable in *The Message*: "How can I picture God's kingdom for you? What kind of story can I use? It's like a pine nut that a man plants in his front yard. It grows into a huge pine tree with thick branches, and eagles build nests in it" (Luke 13:18–19). Having grown up in western Canada, a land with its share of towering pines and majestic eagles, I find this image a much more effective explanation of kingdom growth given my background experience and context. With the image of a majestic pine tree I experience the same "Aha!" moment that was experienced by Jesus' original audience. Creating those "Aha!" moments is what it means to tailor one's accommodation to one's audience.

Clearly an accommodation can be more or less successful. If you seek to accommodate an idea with images that are not actually familiar to the other person, then your attempted accommodation is actually a misfire. For instance, if you asked me what Korean kimchi tastes like, I could try explaining it by comparing it to sauerkraut sprinkled with chili pepper. But the comparison would only be helpful if you knew what sauerkraut was. Otherwise you might completely misunderstand: "*Sour crowd*? So kimchi is like a group of miserable people sprinkled with chili pepper?" Now *that* would be a misfire! As bad as a misfire is, sometimes an attempted accommodation does something worse: it *backfires*. This happens when the accommodation not only fails to connect but actually deepens the misunderstanding by conveying a false, misleading or harmful impression.

This brings me finally to the metaphor of God as Father. *Everybody* knows what fathers are, so this image is in no danger of misfiring. Right? Indeed, the idea of God as Father has resonated with generations of Christians based on their experience of their own fathers as protectors, mentors, friends, and providers (Luke 11:11). Mack's wife Nan is an excellent example, as her close and intimate relationship with her father provided her with a context to experience God as Father (38). As a result, Mack explained to his new friends while on their camping trip, "She thinks about God differently than most folks. She even calls him Papa because of the closeness of their relationship, if that makes sense" (37). This image powerfully communicates God's love and care to Nan. As such, it is hardly surprising that "Papa was Nan's favorite name for God and it expressed her delight in the intimate friendship she had with him" (22).

But the unfortunate reality is that many people have not had a loving human father, and Mack was one of them. Indeed, as a child he constantly lived in fear of his abusive, alcoholic father, culminating in his futile attempt to report his father's abuse to authorities. Upon discovering his son's attempted mutiny, Mack's father retaliated by tying the boy to a tree and beating him for two days "with a belt and Bible verses" (8). Those horrifying experiences have ensured that the image of God as Father, which speaks so powerfully to Nan, viciously backfires on Mack. The attempt to think of God as Father blasts Mack with all the pain, rage and fear that he experienced as a young child.

To get a sense of Mack's adverse reaction to the metaphor, think of a child who contracts the stomach flu immediately after eating strawberry shortcake. Suddenly that child is utterly repulsed by strawberry shortcake. Indeed, the very thought of it is enough to make her retch. Now she simply cannot conceive of eating a dessert that is loved by children the world over. And so it is with Mack's view of God as Father. That image, which is beloved of so many, is now for him utterly repugnant.

This brings us to the real tragedy: although he cannot think of a loving God as Father, this is the central image that Mack has been given, time and again, in the Bible and church. Is it any surprise that rather than finding this image fostering an intimate relationship with God, he has come to view God as "brooding, distant, and aloof" (10)? And so when Sarah, one of Mack's camping neighbors on that fateful weekend, asks whether anyone else in the family calls God Papa, Mack responds: "The kids have picked it up some, but I'm not comfortable with it. It just seems a little too familiar for me. Anyway, Nan has a wonderful father, so I think it's just easier for her" (38). Mack has never had *anyone* he could call Papa (91), and so he cannot now begin to think of God in these terms. Tragically, when Papa offers to be *Mack's* Papa, Mack finds the offer "at once inviting and at the same time repulsive" (92). Is this not all sadly ironic, that the very image which God intended as the path for accommodating relationship has become for Mack an insurmountable obstacle?

So what hope is there for Mack? In answer to this question I am reminded of a story about Pope John XXIII. In 1958 the Vatican got more than they had bargained for when John

XXIII was voted in as the 261st pope of the Roman Catholic Church. Immediately this jolly and humble man began to break with convention, while causing his cardinals no small amount of worry in the process.

In one egregious violation of Vatican protocol, John insisted on visiting the jailed prisoners of Rome with the explanation that because they could not come see him, he came to see them! I love that story because it reminds me of the way that God too comes to meet people who, locked in painful prisons of personal history, are unable to come see him. In meeting people where they are, Pope John was doing nothing more than what he had learned from Paul who became all things to all people so that he might save some (1 Corinthians 9:22). Paul did nothing that he did not learn from Jesus, that exemplar of God's deep accommodation to human limitations. Jesus came because he was sent by God his Father (John 3:16) as an expression of the Father's heart of accommodation.

So is it any surprise that the same God that has always met us where we are comes to meet Mack in his prison as well? Papa is not unaware of Mack's struggles and his pain. She knows that his alienation from her traces to his own abusive father: "And after what you've been through, you couldn't very well handle a father right now, could you?" (93). So, just as John was driven by love to pick up his papal robes and sashay into Rome's darkest prisons, so Papa now adopts the form of a loving mother to meet Mack in his dark prison. She gently informs him, "If I choose to *appear* to you as a man or a woman, it's because I love you" (93).

As incredible as this is, the most amazing part of the story is yet to come. Unlike the pope who cannot release anybody from prison, Papa not only meets Mack in his prison but then works to free him from it. With motherly care, Papa begins to work with Jesus and Sarayu to renovate Mack's heart and remove the roadblocks that have impeded his ability to embrace her as Father. The final moment of healing comes unexpectedly on Saturday after Sarayu brings Mack to a mysterious meadow. Here a wonderful scene begins to unfold. First children spill into the meadow, their frolicking forms accented with brilliant auras displaying the vivid life of the new creation. Gradually a large circle of adults encircles the playing children and then beyond them emerges a ring of angels. Then suddenly the euphoric scene is broken as one of the adults begins to show distress which becomes visible through the violent flashes of his aura. When Mack enquires as to this fellow's problem, Sarayu explains that the man is Mack's father. This man, who had once been Mack's worst nightmare, is now consumed by guilt and remorse for the pain he caused his son. With this revelation, Mack is overcome by emotion and the desire for reconciliation. And so he breaks out into the meadow and runs to meet his father like "a little boy wanting his daddy" (215). With tears running down his cheeks, Mack takes his father's face in his hands and offers forgiveness. As they embrace, he at last receives the human papa he had so long desired.

Now that he has been healed, Mack is no longer repulsed by the image of fatherhood. Indeed, rather than backfiring, he can now see in this image something of the love and care that reflects the heart of God. This leads to yet another surprise for Mack. When he awakens on Sunday morning, Papa the woman is not to be found. Instead, Mack meets a grandfatherly persona, though one rather more striking and rugged than his familiar Gandalf image: "He had silver-white hair pulled back into a ponytail, matched by a gray-splashed mustache and goatee. Plaid shirt with sleeves rolled up, jeans, and hiking boots completed the outfit of someone ready to hit the trail. 'Papa?' Mack asked" (218). Indeed, since Mack has forgiven his human father he can now experience God as Father (221). With his beloved God as Father Mack is ready for the painful journey ahead in which (as yet unbeknownst to Mack), he will retrieve Missy's body for a proper burial. Since Mack will need his heavenly Father to strengthen him through this new ordeal, this is the way that Papa has come to him (219).

Is There Room for a Mother God?

Evangelicals have typically been dismissive of (or even hostile to) attempts to describe God with female analogies and metaphors. Often the complaint is that such concerns reflect political correctness run amok or even the infiltration of a dangerous feminist agenda. But Mack's experience raises a critical urgency to the question. Mack demonstrates that it is not only women with an ideological axe to grind who are reluctant to call God Father. There are also many people (women *and men*) who have experienced deep pain at the hands of abusive males.

Some, like Mack, have been terrorized by human fathers. Others have been sexually abused by "father" priests. And still others have only the vaguest memory of a father who long ago abandoned the family. Perhaps in some cases the light of God as Father can break through these bleak histories. But what if the image of God as Father continues to hover like an ominous cloud on their horizon, blocking out the light of God's love? Must one remain with this image which, far from fostering intimacy, has become a painful obstacle?

We can begin to address this question by considering relevant Scriptures. While there is no doubt that the Bible is heavily weighted to male analogies and metaphors, there is a smattering of female and maternal figures of speech to be found. To begin with, God is likened to a mother: "As a mother comforts her child, so will I comfort you; and you will be comforted over Jerusalem" (Isaiah 66:13). In the New Testament God implicitly assumes a female role in Jesus' parables of a woman mixing yeast into dough (Matthew 13:33) and a woman's search for a lost coin (Luke 15:8–9). The maternal properties of animals are applied to God when he is described as being like a bear robbed of her cubs (Hosea 13:8), while Jesus compares his concern for Jerusalem to a hen longing to gather her chicks (Matthew 23:37).

Speaking of Jesus, many Christians have interpreted the character of Wisdom through whom God made the world in Proverbs 8:22–36 as an Old Testament reference to Christ. The New Testament supports this interpretation since it claims that God created all things through Christ (John 1:3; 1 Corinthians 8:6; Colossians 1:16; Hebrews 1:2). In addition, Jesus refers to himself as the wisdom of God (Matthew 11:19), a confession which is echoed by Paul (1 Corinthians 1:24). The idea of Jesus as the divine wisdom is striking since the word for wisdom in both Hebrew and Greek is feminine (in Hebrew: *hokmah*; in Greek: *sophia*). Could it be that Sophia, the shadowy female figure who interrogates Mack in the cave as the personification of God's wisdom, is actually Jesus appearing in female form? *The Shack* offers no final clarity on the point, but it is an intriguing speculation.

So we return to our question. Is it ever appropriate to think of God as Mother or to pray "Our Mother, who art in heaven . . ."? *The Shack* offers us no settled position on this question. But it does challenge the human tendency to become entrenched in one narrow set of images for God. If we become too committed to one or another image of God, it can become an idol for ourselves and a stumbling block for others.

So how far do you think God will go to meet people in the midst of their suffering? *The Shack* suggests that it is much farther than we could ever have imagined.

DIGGING DEEPER

(1) How does somebody decide which descriptions in Scripture are anthropomorphic and which are not? What about descriptions of God as having human emotion? Does God really get angry, suffer, and love us, or are these accommodations to the human emotional life?

(2) Given that Jesus taught us to address God in prayer as "Our

Father" (Matthew 6:9) is it improper for someone to pray to God as Mother?

(3) How would you advise someone who, like Mack, felt alienated from God the Father because of an abusive human father?

(4) What sort of images of God do you find most comfortable?

(5) Given that Christians have long embraced multi-ethnic portrayals of Jesus, is it ever permissible to depict Jesus as a woman? If not, then why not?

CHAPTER 3

The Mystery of Three in One

Being a theologian is often a thankless task. Take the case of Apollinaris. One of the greatest theologians of the fourth century, and a staunch defender of orthodoxy, he nonetheless ended life branded a heretic. His crime? He had dared develop an account of the incarnation which was deemed inadequate by his peers. And so with the dreaded *H* word (heresy), a whole lifetime of diligent work for the church could be overshadowed.

Within Christianity there are few words that cut to the quick as sharply as *heresy*. And *The Shack* has certainly been charged with its share of heresies. Perhaps the most serious of these concerns is a view that we have already touched upon: modalism. To recap, according to modalism God is not three distinct persons but rather one person who acts in three roles in history. On this view, God is like an actor who dons three different masks during his performance. In this way, God first acts as the Father and then as the Son and finally as the Spirit. Given that modalism has been denounced as a heresy since the early third century, it is no small matter that *The Shack* has been charged with this theological error. But before we allow this book's contributions to be overshadowed, we must consider whether the dreaded *H* word is a legitimate charge?

In fact, the critic can marshal an impressive list of texts in support of the charge. Consider first Papa's description of the incarnation: "When we three spoke ourself into human existence as the Son of God, we became fully human. We also chose to embrace all the limitations that this entailed. Even though we have always been present in this created universe, we now became flesh and blood" (99; see also 100 and 201). Rather than affirm that God's Son became incarnate (John 1:14), this passage seems to suggest that the Father, Son, and Spirit all became incarnate, as if all three squeezed into the developing body of Jesus in Mary's womb! But surely this bizarre notion cannot be correct. So is there another interpretation of Papa's words? The other obvious possibility is that Papa is meaning to affirm that the three persons are really one person who incarnated as Jesus. Unfortunately, this more plausible interpretation is modalistic.

Is there any other evidence to support the modalist interpretation of *The Shack*? Consider that Papa says, "I am God.

I am who I am" (97). In other words, Papa claims for herself the unique name of God (Exodus 3:14). To complicate matters, later Sarayu claims the same name for herself: "I am that I am. I will be who I will be!" (204). But if there is one I AM, and both Papa and Sarayu claim to be the I AM, then are not Papa and Sarayu one and the same person?

This matter is of no small concern, for as I said in the first chapter, the doctrine of the Trinity is an essential mark of Christian identity. Deny it and you are labeled with that ugly word "heretic." So is there enough evidence in *The Shack* to convict the book of heresy? While I admit that the reference to the three speaking themselves into existence is unfortunate, in this chapter I shall argue that once we understand the doctrine of the Trinity and *The Shack*'s subtle presentation of it, we will see that the book is not heretical at all. In fact, it presents a stimulating articulation of what Christians *should* believe about God! Indeed, when all the evidence is in, we will be left to wonder how the critics could have ever drawn their conclusions to begin with.

The Paradoxical Trinity in Scripture

One of my problems with some of the critics of *The Shack* is that they have criticized tensions in the book's depiction of God without ever acknowledging similar tensions in the Bible's depiction of God.

As such, we need to begin by noting that many critics of Christianity have charged the doctrine of the Trinity with being contradictory. After all, Trinitarians claim that there are three divine and distinct persons, Father, Son, and Spirit, but yet there is only one God. This led eighteenth century Unitarian Joseph Priestley to complain that the claim that Father, Son, and Spirit are one God "is certainly as much a contradiction, as to say that Peter, James, and John, having each of them every thing that is requisite to constitute a complete man, are yet altogether not three men, but only one man."[1] According to critics like Priestley, if Christians are going to recognize three divine beings then they should come out and admit that they really are trithe-ists (that is, that they believe there are three gods)! It is merely stubborn, muddled thinking that allows them to insist that they are monotheists.

Priestley has a legitimate argument. So why did the church ever adopt a doctrine that appears to be contradictory? The question is especially pressing since Christianity is not like some religious traditions (e.g., Zen Buddhism) that deliberately em-brace paradoxes of reason as a way to clear the mind for mystical enlightenment. On the contrary, Christians have generally taken reason very seriously. As a result, they recognize that an appar-ently contradictory doctrine is not a trivial matter. But even so, they find themselves driven to affirm each of the core doctrinal affirmations of the Trinity that, when taken together, appear to lead to a contradiction. That is, they believe that Scripture affirms that there is one God, that the Father, Son, and Spirit are God, and that the Father, Son, and Spirit are distinct. Let's take

---

1. Joseph Priestley, *The Theological and Miscellaneous Works of Joseph Priestley,* ed. John Towil Rutt (No Place: G. Smallfield, 1786), 34.

a moment to consider some of the biblical evidence for each of these claims.

There is one God. This is the simplest confession to establish, for monotheism is the consistent teaching of Scripture (Exodus 3:14; Isaiah 44:6) and was never questioned by the early Christians (1 Corinthians 8:6; James 2:19).

The Father, Son, and Spirit are God. Throughout the New Testament the title God is consistently applied to the Father (e.g., Matthew 6:9; 1 Corinthians 8:6). But is there also evidence for the deity of the Son and Spirit? Jesus is explicitly identified as God in a few key passages including John 1:1, 1:18, and Thomas' incredible confession in John 20:28 where he declares to Jesus, "My Lord and my God!" Other passages refer to the divinity of Christ including Romans 9:5, Colossians 1:15 and 2:9, and Hebrews 1:10–12 where the writer applies the description of Yahweh in Psalm 102:25–27 to Jesus. But my single favorite example of a Scripture for Christ's deity comes in the enigmatic book of Revelation: while the Lord God proclaims himself the "Alpha and Omega" in 1:8 (compare Isaiah 44:6), later in 22:13 Jesus describes himself as the Alpha and Omega, the beginning and end (compare Hebrews 13:8). With this divine title, we find a truly beautiful revelation of Christ's full divinity coming at the final climax of all Scripture! In addition to these texts the early Christians directed prayers (Acts 7:59–60; 1 Corinthians 16:22; 2 Corinthians 12:8; Revelation 22:20) and praises (Hebrews 13:21; 2 Peter 3:18) to Jesus. Indeed, God *commands* his angels to worship Christ (Hebrews 1:6) and in Revelation we see a vision of every creature in heaven and earth praising God *and* the

Lamb (5:13)! When one considers that all these affirmations are being made by recent converts from Judaism, the most vigorously monotheistic religion the world has ever known, the effect is simply staggering! Somehow the early followers of Jesus were driven to recognize his equal deity to the Father even as they continued to maintain their commitment to monotheism.

There is little doubt that the Scriptures portray the Spirit as fully divine, for he is the Spirit of God (Matthew 3:16) and of Christ (Romans 8:9). In addition, the one unforgiveable sin is blaspheming the Spirit (Mark 3:29) and lying to the Spirit is equivalent to lying to God (Acts 5:3–4). Thus much of the early Spirit debate was instead concerned with whether the Spirit was a distinct person. The problem arose because the word "spirit" may also be translated as breath, and "breath of God" sounds like it belongs in the same anthropomorphic category as hand of the LORD (Exodus 7:5) and eyes of the LORD (Genesis 18:3,10). (Nobody is inclined to confess the Father, Son, and *eyes* of God, so why would one confess Father, Son, and Spirit/breath of God?) Nonetheless, the church concluded that the Spirit was not merely an anthropomorphic description of God breathing but instead was a distinct person.

One excellent reason to believe the Spirit is a person is because Jesus did. After all, Jesus promised the Spirit as *another* comforter (that means, another like Jesus, one of the same kind) who would come in his absence (John 14:16–17). If Jesus is a divine person, then this implies another divine person to come. This interpretation is reinforced by the fact that Jesus refers to the Spirit not with the grammatically appropriate pronoun "it," but rather the personal "he" as in "he will testify about me" (John 15:26) and "he will guide you into all the truth" (John 16:13). This is *not* how you describe breath! Not surprisingly, the early church experienced the Spirit as a personal reality who spoke to and guided the apostles (Acts 9:31, 13:2).

The Father, Son, and Spirit are distinct. Finally, we turn to a large number of New Testament texts that clearly distinguish the persons. For instance, during the baptism of Jesus the Father spoke from heaven and the Spirit descended as a dove (Luke 3:21–22). Given the distinct roles that the Father, Son, and Spirit all played in this single event, it appears rather implausible to suppose that the baptism consisted of one divine person simultaneously assuming all three roles! Indeed, the three persons repeatedly distinguish themselves from one another as when Jesus prayed to the Father in Gethsemane and promised the Spirit in the upper room. In addition, we could add numerous other passages where the persons are clearly distinguished (see Matthew 28:19–20; 1 Corinthians 12:4–6; 2 Corinthians 13:14; Ephesians 2:18; 1 Peter 1:2–12; Jude 20–21; Revelation 1:4–5).

This evidence suggests that far from setting out to concoct an apparently contradictory doctrine, Christians were forced to this set of affirmations by the New Testament revelation itself. But while this may indeed be the witness of Scripture, it does not diminish the fact that it appears to entail a contradictory affirmation that one equals three! While Christians admit the problem, instead of conceding that the teaching is contradictory, they explain it as a paradox (that is, an *apparent* contradiction).

Three points support this claim. First, the doctrine of the Trinity is not stated in a straightforwardly contradictory manner. That is, Christians do not say that "the one God is three Gods." That *would* be contradictory. Rather, they claim that the one God is three *persons*. While this maneuver may be insufficient to guarantee the coherence of the doctrine, it is sufficient to avoid an overt contradiction.[2]

Of course some people will remain skeptical, believing that Christians are just trying to hide a contradictory claim with an appeal to paradox. This brings us to our second point: that even highly rational and rigorous disciplines like mathematics and the science of quantum physics admit of many paradoxes that are accepted by the specialists in each discipline.[3] But if mathematicians and physicists can rationally accept paradoxes based on their data sets, surely theologians may as well. Should it surprise us that there is much in heaven and earth that we cannot fully understand? As the great mathematician and apologist Blaise Pascal observed, "Reason's final step is to recognize that there is an infinity of things beyond it."[4] Indeed, Willie makes a similar point in *The Shack* when he suggests that certain mysteries may

---

2. For a survey of some of the attempts Christian theologians have pursued to explain the doctrine's coherence see my *Faith Lacking Understanding* (Carlisle: Paternoster, 2008), ch. 2.
3. For an overview of paradoxes related to mathematical infinity see the introduction to A.W. Moore, *The Infinite* (London and New York: Routledge, 1990).
4. Blaise Pascal, *Pensées,* ed. and trans. Roger Ariew (Indianapolis/ Cambridge: Hackett Publishing Co., 2005), 55.

only be comprehensible in a realm of "suprarationality" that transcends our puny minds (67).

Finally, we come to our third point: if there is any place in all human knowledge where we would expect to encounter paradoxes, it would surely be in our attempt to understand God! Remember in chapter two that we noted a central attribute of God is infinity, his absolute transcendence over our concepts. But then Christianity appears to posit a paradox *right where we would expect to encounter one,* in the doctrine of God! From that perspective, it may well be that the paradox we face is not so much a problem as a sign that we *really are* grappling with the infinite God! As Papa observes, "Who wants to worship a God who can be fully comprehended, eh? Not much mystery in that" (101).

Is *The Shack* Modalistic?

One could concede that the Scriptures present a mystery and still argue that *The Shack* blunders off the trail of mystery and into the briars of modalistic heresy. The initial problem with that charge, based as it is upon a few passages from *The Shack*, is that one could also quote selectively from Scripture to support modalism. For instance, the familiar messianic prophecy in Isaiah 9:6 describes the child to be born as both "Everlasting Father" *and* "Prince of Peace." But wait! This seems to suggest that Jesus, the Prince of Peace, is the same individual as the Everlasting Father, and this implies modalism! In addition, Jesus' claim that he is one with the Father (John 10:10) could be interpreted as meaning that they are one and the same person. The same interpretation could be derived from Jesus' claim that whoever has seen him has seen the Father (John 14:9). So Scripture can be used to develop a case for modalism! However, before you panic, be assured that it is not a good case. This list ignores both the context of the relevant passages as well as the wider testimony of Scripture.

So now the obvious question: if even Scripture can be selectively quoted in favor of modalism, what about *The Shack*? Is there evidence that the critics have developed an erroneous case based on a few problem texts? In response, let's begin with a point so obvious that it could easily be overlooked. One way we argue against modalism in Scripture is rooted in the repeated distinction of Father, Son, and Spirit in the biblical narrative (e.g., in Jesus' baptism). By the same token, the fact that *The Shack* repeatedly distinguishes Papa, Jesus, and Sarayu likewise counts against modalism. Indeed, on *multiple* occasions Mack is simultaneously present with Papa, Jesus, and Sarayu (frequently sharing a communal feast), and he watches them interact with intimacy and love. If this is one God simply playing three simultaneous roles, then it is quite the unique (and misleading) party trick!

Let us now consider the problematic point where Papa seems to say the three become incarnate as one. The one thing we should observe here is that Mack does not understand this to imply modalism. Rather, Papa's statement prompts Mack to puzzle over the mysterious relations of the Trinity: "There's that whole Trinity thing, which is where I kind of get lost" (100). Sure Mack may get lost when he thinks about the Trinity, but then he's just like the rest of us. The important point is that here as elsewhere the book opts for mystery rather than modalism.

If one ever needed a good sign that *The Shack* is not modalistic, one would find it in the fact that other critics have charged it with the exact opposite error of tritheism! These critics worry that there is *too much* distinction in Papa, Jesus, and Sarayu and so they must be three gods! But surely these two charges cancel one another out! In fact, *The Shack* clearly rejects both modalism and tritheism. As Papa says, "We are not three gods, and we are not talking about one god with three attitudes, like a man who is a husband, father, and worker. I am one God and I am three persons, and each of the three is fully and entirely the one" (101). To hammer the point home, Papa then goes on to explain that if modalism were in fact true then God could not be loving in his own being. Since God is loving in his own being, he must be Trinity! The mystery of the Trinity is undoubtedly great: how could it be that Papa, Jesus, and Sarayu are three distinct and fully divine persons, and yet there is only one God? However we work this out, we should take *The Shack*'s advice and embrace mystery rather than heresy.

Is *The Shack* just confused?

Perhaps the critic ought to concede that *The Shack* is not really modalistic, but could the book just be confused? Could it be that *The Shack* does not really know what it believes? Indeed, perhaps the mixed signals of identity and distinction which prompt contradictory charges simply arise from this confusion. In fact, I would argue that the tension between one and three that exists in *The Shack* is a sign of good biblical theology. This will become clear if we turn back to the Scriptures, for it is here that the tension between the one and three is rooted.

I'll give three examples. Let's begin with the "Angel of the LORD" passages in the Old Testament, for these have long puzzled interpreters (see for instance Genesis 16:7–13; Exodus 3:2–6). The mystery lies in the fact that that whenever the Angel of the LORD appears, it is both distinguished from God and identified with God. For instance, immediately after the Angel of the LORD halts Abraham from carrying through his sacrifice of Isaac, the Angel calls to Abraham, though it is the Lord who speaks: "I swear by myself, declares the Lord, that because you have done this and have not withheld your son, your only son, I will surely bless you" (Genesis 22:16–17). But how can it be that when the Angel of the LORD speaks it is God who speaks? Is the angel really God or distinct from God? Certainly the angel cannot be both?

As we continue to mull over that puzzle, we find a very similar mystery at the very beginning of John's gospel: "The Word was with God, and the Word was God" (John 1:1). Here the "Word" is Jesus. And so John seems to be saying that the Word both is God and yet is distinct from God at the same time. But how can this be? How can the Word *be with* God and also *be* God? While this mystery remains with us, it is interesting to note that many theologians in the early church linked the puzzling Angel of the LORD passages with Jesus by arguing that the Angel was Jesus before the incarnation! (One finds implicit support for this claim in the fact that the Angel of the LORD makes no appearance in the New Testament, perhaps because he is now in our midst as Jesus.)

Finally, let us consider one more difficult passage, this one in the writings of Paul: "Now the Lord is the Spirit. . . . And we all, who with unveiled faces contemplate the Lord's glory, are being transformed into his image with ever-increasing glory, which comes from the Lord, who is the Spirit" (2 Corinthians 3:17–18). This is puzzling because elsewhere Paul clearly distinguishes Jesus and the Holy Spirit (Romans 15:30; 1 Corinthians 6:11). In fact he does so later in this very letter (2 Corinthians 13:14)! And yet in the two verses cited above he seems to *identify* Jesus and the Spirit. How do we explain these apparently contradictory statements concerning the Angel of the LORD, God, Jesus, and the Spirit?

The interesting thing about the biblical passages in question is that they reflect a tension very much like the one present within *The Shack*. This is the tension between affirming the identity of three distinct persons within the one God while avoiding both modalism and tritheism. Throughout Scripture, and particularly in the New Testament, there is an attempt to affirm both the identity and distinction. Remember that Papa and Sarayu claim for themselves the one divine name "I AM." Is this evidence of modalism? Certainly no more so than when Jesus claims the one divine name in John 8:58, "Before Abraham was born, I AM!" And let us not forget that Jesus commends his disciples to baptize in the (singular) *name* of Father, Son, and Spirit (Matthew 28:19). In other words, *The Shack*'s patterns of identity and distinction trace back to prior patterns within Scripture.

Given the mysterious nature of the biblical witness, how should Christians state the doctrine of the Trinity? If we are concerned to avoid heresy, what should we say that we believe? Consider again Papa's definition: "I am one God and I am three persons, and each of the three is fully and entirely the one" (101). It is fascinating to observe that this statement is actually quite similar to some very influential formal statements of the doctrine of the Trinity. Consider the Catholic Church's influential Fourth Lateran Council of 1215 which defined the Trinity as "one supreme reality . . . incomprehensible and ineffable, which is truly Father, Son and Holy Spirit; at once the three persons taken together and each of them singly."[5] This is exactly what *The Shack* says! As both definitions remind us, we must be careful not to think of the Father, Son, and Spirit as three parts of the one God. Rather, each fully is the one God and yet they are distinct and there is one God. Many of *The Shack*'s critics would do well if they could articulate this mystery as well as the book they criticize!

Contemplating the Trinity can certainly be a disorienting affair as you are constantly being drawn between thinking about God as one and as three. You see this when Philip, upon asking Jesus to see the Father, is informed that he is seeing the Father in Jesus (John 14:9). You see it when the early Christians are warned that lying to the Holy Spirit is lying to God (Acts 5:4).

---

5. Cited in David Brown, *The Divine Trinity* (London: Duckworth, 1985), 242.

And you see it when Mack has a conversation with Papa about limitation and then later Sarayu refers back to the conversation as if *she* had been speaking with him (106)! This is not modalism because Mack then turns to Papa confused, and Papa looks back at him knowingly (that is, Papa and Sarayu are different). But it is a subtle reference to the dynamism between the one and three. The beautiful oscillation between the unity and distinction is evident when Mack first meets the three and asks which of them is God: "'I am,' said all three in unison. Mack looked from one to the next, and even though he couldn't begin to grasp what he was seeing and hearing, he somehow believed them" (87). And finally, we see it near the end of Mack's stay when, at Missy's memorial, Sarayu sings Missy's song and then "God, all three, simultaneously said, 'Amen'" (233). Perhaps no theologian has described this dizzying experience of the triune God as well as the fourth century theologian Gregory Nazianzen:

> No sooner do I conceive of the One than I am illumined by the splendour of the Three; no sooner do I distinguish Them than I am carried back to the One. When I think of any One of the Three, I think of him as the whole, and my eyes are filled, and the greater part of what I am thinking of escapes me. I cannot grasp the greatness of that One so as to attribute a greater greatness to the rest. When I contemplate the Three together, I see but one torch, and cannot divide or measure out the undivided light.[6]

---

6. Cited in Vladimir Lossky, *The Mystical Theology of the Eastern Church* (Crestwood, NY: St. Vladimir's Seminary Press, 1976), 46.

This same dynamic mystery pervades the Scriptures as lowly human beings meet the infinitely mysterious Three-in-One. And so it is an ever present reality for Mack during his unforgettable weekend.

The Shack's nuanced portrayal of the three divine persons extends to the unique way the narrative identifies the distinct characteristics of each. As such, we shall end the chapter with a reflection on the very different revelations of Sarayu and Jesus.

Meeting the Mystery of Sarayu

Having been raised in the Pentecostal church, I lived for years within a tradition that strongly emphasizes the Holy Spirit. Yet even Pentecostals can struggle with thinking of the Spirit in fully personal terms. I recall one pastor who described how, after a crowd had gathered to receive the Spirit at an altar call, the Spirit roared into the room and then "bounced off one fellow and hit another!" But the Spirit is not like a pinball bouncing around the congregation. While this may have been an unfortunate statement, it reflects the fact that Christians have always struggled to think about the Spirit in personal terms. After all, while the Father and Son are revealed throughout the Scripture in concrete and personal metaphors (with the Son even becoming incarnate), there are no equally concrete and personal images of the Spirit. On the contrary, the most dominant image for the Spirit is that of wind: "The wind blows wherever it pleases. You hear its sound, but you cannot tell where it comes from or where it is going. So it is with everyone born of the Spirit" (John 3:8). The image of wind is intriguing both in what it does and does not reveal of the Spirit. Wind is always in movement and is seen not directly but rather only through its effects in the world. In addition, the concept of wind/breath provides an image that is intimate and penetrating. These characteristics of the wind capture something of the Spirit's action in the world.

The Shack reflects the movement of the Spirit along with the fact that the Spirit is the most intangible of the persons. We read the following of Mack's first encounter with Sarayu:

> As she stepped back, Mack found himself involuntarily squinting in her direction, as if doing so would allow his eyes to see her better. But strangely, he still had a difficult time focusing on her; she seemed almost to shimmer in the light and her hair blew in all directions even though there was hardly a breeze. It was almost easier to see her out of the corner of his eye than it was to look at her directly. (84)

With this image, *The Shack* communicates the dynamism of Sarayu as the wind that is constantly in movement (120). In addition, like the wind she is impossible to perceive directly, as "she seemed to phase in and out of his vision" (85). And so the work of Sarayu remains mysterious and unpredictable, for "like her name, she wafted about like a playful eddying wind and he never quite knew which way she was blowing" (130).

The mystery comes upon us in other surprising ways. Many people who have been present at the death of a loved one describe the sense that something was withdrawn at death. Scientists in the nineteenth century actually had a term for this: they called it the vitalistic life force, and when the force left, death resulted.

Unfortunately this description never caught on as a theory. Perhaps it was too mysterious for the modern scientific mind.

To this day, exactly what occurs at death remains largely mysterious. Biblically speaking, we have an answer: when the Spirit that gives life withdraws that breath, death ensues (Psalm 104:30; Job 34:14–15). As such, the Spirit is radically present to all living things, granting life every moment. Within this light it is fascinating to see how this is reflected when Mack is embraced by Sarayu. Amazingly, she penetrates his very being so that he cannot tell where his body ends and her enlivening presence begins: "Mack suddenly felt lighter than air, almost as if he were no longer touching the ground. She was hugging him without hugging him, or really without even touching him. Only when she pulled back, which was probably just seconds later, did he realize that he was still standing on his feet" (85). Such is the description of one's encounter with the Spirit that gives life to all things and then comes to indwell within the believer.

In addition, the Spirit works to empower and inspire human beings to accomplish various tasks including great works of aesthetic beauty (Exodus 31:1–5). How incredible it is to contemplate the fact that great works of art reflect ways that the Spirit works to mediate beauty and bring glory back to God the Father so that culture may praise God as does creation (Psalm 19:1–2). Sarayu manifests the Spirit's creative and enlivening presence within creation with her role as the keeper of the gardens (87). In addition to her artistry within creation that is manifested in the garden, she reflects her presence within human culture and art by singing Missy's beautiful song (96, 108), an image that is especially profound if Missy's original composition of the song was inspired by the Spirit!

Jesus Christ, Man and Mediator

In contrast to Papa who changes form from female to male as needs may require, and to Sarayu who remains perpetually intangible and mysterious, Mack's encounters with Jesus are strikingly concrete and tangible. Instead of changing form, Jesus remains concretely present as a first century Jewish carpenter with a good sense of humor . . . and rather average looks (84, compare Isaiah 53:2). As a result, Mack naturally finds himself more comfortable around Jesus, for Jesus just seems "more real, or tangible" (110) than Papa or Sarayu. As Mack put it, "It's like I've always known you. But Papa isn't at all what I expected from God, and Sarayu, she's *way* out there" (110). Jesus also acknowledges that he is different from Papa and Sarayu when he explains to Mack: "Since I am human we have much in common to begin with" (110).

So, while Mack initially finds it difficult to relate to the almost over-bearing presence of Papa and the mysterious nature of Sarayu, he always finds Jesus approachable: "He admitted to himself that he liked Jesus a lot, but he seemed the least godlike of the three" (117). The uniquely concrete presence of Jesus becomes manifest in a mundane but striking fashion when Jesus hugs Mack and (contrary to the airy embrace of Sarayu) it actually *feels* like a hug! (85, 219).

With that simple but profound reflection that a hug from Jesus is a real human hug, we enter into one of the greatest mysteries in theology: the incarnation of God the Son as Jesus Christ (John 1:14). Sadly, Christians have often failed to understand the full import of this mystery. It is here that *The Shack* has something very important to show us. To begin with, we need to recognize the full implications of the fact that Christ made himself nothing (Philippians 2:7), and thereby took on the full limitations of humanity. But even when Christians affirm the fullness of the incarnation, they are often unaware of the radical extent of the Christian claim. You see, the incarnation is not simply an anomalous event that occurred for a span of about three decades some two millennia ago, but rather *it remains a living reality today!* Jesus did not leave his humanity behind when he ascended back to heaven. Rather, he ascended to the right hand of the Father as the eternally incarnate God-Man (1 Timothy 2:5).

If this is what Christians are *supposed* to believe, then why do so many Christians apparently believe that Jesus eventually sloughed off his humanity? I suspect that many assume that when Jesus was exalted to the highest place (Philippians 2:9) he must have left his humanity behind. But in fact Scripture *nowhere* suggests that Christ's exaltation entailed the end of the incarnation. On the contrary, Christ had a fully human resurrection body (Luke 24:38–43; John 20:26–29), and he ascended embodied to the right hand of the Father (Luke 24:51). He will return in this same way (Acts 1:11) as the Son of Man (Matthew 16:27). The great mystery of God the Son taking on the humble human estate continues when the incarnate Son then exalts his humanity back into the divine.

Even if Christ is eternally incarnate, one might reasonably wonder what difference this makes. To illustrate, let's think of the contrast between a person going for a two week short-term mission among India's Dalits (otherwise known as the untouchables, India's lowest socio-economic class) and another person going to work with the Dalits for the rest of his life. While we might admire the short-term missionary's commitment (that's not the way *I'd* want to spend my vacation!) there simply is a different order of commitment with the lifetime missionary. We cannot even conceive of giving our whole lives for such a service. Years after the first missionary has returned to his North American life, the second missionary will continue to labor among the Dalits. Now *that* shows a uniquely profound love for this people.

This is what the incarnation entails. How incredible that Christ's extraordinary identification with the human condition is like the second missionary! Consider that just as the second missionary continues to work for the Dalits, so even now Christ continues to work as mediator before the Father (1 Timothy 2:5). This does not undermine Jesus' once for all sacrifice on the cross but rather reflects the fact that he continues to work as our mediator in the application of that atoning work to our lives. The writer to the Hebrews explains further: "Therefore he is able to save completely those who come to God through him, because he always lives to intercede for them" (Hebrews 7:25). And so, just as it was crucial that Christ undertake his atoning work as fully God and fully man, so it remains important that his mediating work continues to be carried out as "fully God and fully man." The incredible result, as Paul explains, is that we may approach God with freedom and confidence through faith in Christ (Ephesians 3:12).

Is there a way that we might render this concept of Christ's ongoing mediatorial role more concrete? To answer this question we can turn to the topic of prayer. On his unforgettable weekend Mack rightly puzzles over the idea of praying for the meal when his three table companions are the Father, Son, and Holy Spirit. But few people can claim to have sat down with one (or more) persons of the Trinity for dinner. For most of us, the normative way of communing with God is through prayer, and so it is important to understand the proper form of prayer.

How is prayer taught and modeled in the New Testament? While there are four places in the New Testament where prayers are directed to Christ (cited above), these do not appear to be normative for the church. Rather, as a regular practice Jesus taught us to pray to the Father (Matthew 6:9), and this direction for prayer was taken up in the early church (Acts 12:5; Colossians 1:3). While prayers are directed to the Father, Christ is the mediator of our prayers, the one *through whom* we pray to the Father: "Through Jesus, therefore, let us continually offer to God a sacrifice of praise—the fruit of lips that openly profess his name" (Hebrews 13:15). It is only because of the work of Christ that we are called children of God and thus can approach the Father of Jesus in prayer as *our* Father. As a result, while praying to Jesus is certainly proper since he is God, if we only pray to

Jesus we tend to lose the fact that his work is to mediate our prayers to the Father.[7]

The life of prayer is but one way that Jesus continues as the mediator of our relationship with God. As Mack discovers the concrete and approachable presence of Jesus, he is being brought into encounter with the wonderful mystery that Christ remains our mediator to the Father. It is through his intimate conversation with Jesus that Mack is brought back to Papa where he ultimately finds forgiveness and the restoration of relationship.

DIGGING DEEPER

(1) Do you think that the doctrine of the Trinity makes a difference in the spiritual life of your church or in your personal devotions?

(2) Do you find one of the three persons easier to approach than others? If so, why?

(3) What do you think of the notion that Jesus Christ has eternally identified with the human condition?

(4) How you would respond to the claim that the doctrine of the Trinity is contradictory?

---

7. See Alan Torrance, "Being of One Substance with the Father," in Christopher Seitz, ed., *Nicene Christianity: The Future For a New Ecumenism* (Grand Rapids, MI: Brazos Press, 2001), 59.

CHAPTER 4

GOD WITH NOBODY IN CHARGE

L et's play a word association game. When you hear the word *God*, what descriptors spring into your mind? If you're like most people you think of words like "sovereign," "powerful," "stern," "absolute," and "mighty." Based on this perspective, you might expect an encounter with God to be distinctively awesome, perhaps marked by flashes of lightning, peals of thunder, howling winds . . . and a fair degree of knee-knocking terror. (See Exodus 19:16–19 for a sampling.)

As such, it is all the more surprising that the first sign of God's presence in the shack is not extreme weather conditions, but rather the warm and inviting sound of *laughter!* (81). If this is a surprise to Mack, his perplexity only deepens when he first meets those three tittering characters. Unsure of their identity, he asks whether more persons may be expected: "The three looked at one another and laughed. 'No, Mackenzie,' chuckled the black woman. 'We is all that you get, and believe me, we're more than enough" (85). The whole tone of the conversation is wrong: these people are too goofy to be God! Mack's initial shock only deepens as he witnesses the casual, intimate, and apparently very undivine way that the three interact with one another in relaxed, often humorous, and generally delightful exchanges. Thus, while Moses is warned that no one can look upon God's face and live (Exodus 33:20), Mack has no problem peering directly at the three "with silly grins plastered to their faces" (200). And in contrast to the image of God hidden in the swirling clouds and crashing thunder of Mt. Sinai, the only divine crash Mack hears is when Jesus fumbles in the kitchen:

> Jesus had dropped a large bowl of some sort of batter or sauce on the floor, and it was everywhere. It must have landed close to Papa because the lower portion of her skirt and bare feet were covered in the gooey mess. All three were laughing so hard that Mack didn't think they were breathing. Sarayu said something about humans being clumsy and all three started roaring again. (104)

By this point it has become manifestly evident that *The Shack* intends to give the classic "high" view of God a thorough retooling.

In place of the distant sovereign Lord we now meet what a friend of mine refers to as "the giggling Godhead," a surprisingly approachable, laid back, and generally mirthful deity.

What is perhaps most surprising about God in the shack is that this retooled image is not simply offered as a supplement or counterbalance to the familiar exalted notion. Indeed, there is little if any evidence in the book of the God described by our word association game. That absence seems to be intentional, for at the heart of *The Shack*'s depiction of God is a rejection of the traditional conception of a monarch ruling over a submissive creation. In this chapter we will take a closer look at the book's depiction of God and in particular its rejection of any notion of hierarchy in God. As we will see, *The Shack* offers a rethinking of these concepts which is radical and far-reaching. Whether or not one ultimately agrees with the depiction, it provides an intriguing illustration of the way one's doctrine of the Trinity can powerfully shape one's view of the world.

Thinking about the Giggling God

The depiction of a laughing God has elicited responses no less polarized than those prompted by the image of Papa as an African-American woman. Some have embraced the image of an intimate, laughing God as a liberating and refreshing challenge to the picture of God as angry, judgmental, and distant. But others worry that a mirthful, giggling God does not liberate us so much as reflect the distortions of a culture that is widely skeptical of power, authority, and reverence.

Let's begin by considering the extent to which the depiction offers a helpful critique of an overly humorless picture of God. This struck me one day when I visited an art gallery and saw a painting of Christ's triumphal entry to Jerusalem in which Jesus was riding his donkey utterly stone-faced in the midst of an ecstatic crowd! The picture seemed to imply, bizarrely enough, that laughter was somehow beneath Jesus, as if God cannot deign to crack a smile. But where did this strange idea come from? All the evidence suggests that Jesus was very witty and had an excellent sense of humor![1] What's wrong with Jesus telling a silly joke to the apostles around the campfire? Could it be that when Jesus told a joke it was as much a sign of his deity as his humanity?

While one might in principle affirm *The Shack*'s challenge to the image of God as a "dour deity," we could still worry that the book overcompensates for that error when it describes Father, Son, and Spirit as having "silly grins plastered to their faces." Psychoanalyst Jacques Lacan, who was no friend of Christianity, used to refer sarcastically to the deity of religious faith as "good old God." We need to ask whether *The Shack* has yielded implicit support to Lacan by depicting the Trinity as a merry band of jokers. By the same token, does the wider church inadvertently reinforce such withering attitudes when it treats God more like a harmless old groundskeeper than the Lord of the manor? Do we provide unwitting fuel for Lacan's derision when we bend over backward to remove all reverence and awe in a bid for seeker sensitivity? What does it say about our view of God when

---

1. See Earl F. Palmer, *The Humor of Jesus: Source of Laughter in the Bible* (Vancouver: Regent College Publishing, 2001).

pastors officiate in church dressed up as if they were on the way to the beach while congregants recline in padded pews cradling their Starbucks coffee? In short, have we become dangerously casual when gathered in the presence of Almighty God? Donald McCullough observes:

> Visit a church on Sunday morning—almost any will do—and you will likely find a congregation comfortably relating to a deity who fits nicely within precise doctrinal positions, or who lends almighty support to social crusades, or who conforms to individual spiritual experiences. But you will not likely find much awe or sense of mystery. The only sweaty palms will be those of the preacher unsure whether the sermon will go over; the only shaking knees will be those of the soloist about to sing the offertory.[2]

Note that nobody escapes McCullough's criticism for he indicts with equal aplomb evangelicals (those who emphasize doctrinal positions), liberals (those who emphasize social crusades), and charismatics (those who emphasize spiritual experiences). In other words, every tradition can lose a reverent sense of the holy otherness of God. But God is not our buddy, life coach, or (as many contemporary worship songs might suggest) our romantic consort. Surely we can reject the image of God as humorless, autocratic tyrant without needing to reinvent him as court jester!

---

2. Donald McCullough, *The Trivialization of God: The Dangerous Illusion of a Manageable Deity* (Colorado Springs: NavPress, 1995), 13.

Many Christians today might be tempted to dismiss McCullough's complaint as the predictable grumblings of another sullen theologian glowering in the back pew. Away with this churchy old school formality! Christ has liberated us from the pompous formality of religion and left us free to "approach God's throne of grace with confidence" (Hebrews 4:16). That just may mean coming to church dressed in a loud Hawaiian shirt and flip flops. Perhaps. But then it is interesting to observe that McCullough's grumbling is echoed by *atheist* writer Barbara Ehrenreich. In her recent book *Bait and Switch,* a lively exploration of unemployment in America, Ehrenreich visits a job fair at the Mt. Paran Church of God. There she is informed by the speaker (Francois) that the key to getting a job is networking. While Ehrenreich has heard this advice many times before, Francois then advises his audience that they should begin the process by networking . . . with *God!* Though an atheist, Ehrenreich finds this suggestion *religiously offensive,* even ridiculous:

> I'm sorry, this is too much for me. I endured the Norcross Fellowship Lunch as an atheist, but now, at the Mt. Paran Church of God, I discover that I am a believer, and what I believe is this: if the Lord exists, if there is some conscious being whose thought the universe is—some great spinner of galaxies, hurler of meteors, creator and extinguisher of species—if some such being should manifest itself, you do not "network"

with it any more than you would light a cigarette on the burning bush. Francois is guilty of blasphemy.[3]

Where does the idea that we can network with God come from other than the emasculated conception of Lacan's good old God? Could it be that occasionally Christians have become so comfortable with God that, as Ehrenreich charges, they have waded into the dangerous waters of blasphemy?

These are difficult questions and we certainly cannot resolve them here. As for *The Shack*, it may be that the appropriateness of the book's depiction of God depends on who reads the book and what prior conception of deity they bring to it. Some readers may well find themselves in a similar place to Mack. Perhaps they have experienced severe trauma or abuse in their lives and as a result they have come to view God as harsh, distant, and cold. For such people the depiction of God in *The Shack* might indeed be a liberating corrective that redresses excessive distance with the warmth, love, and joy of the triune God. But many others have never agonized over their own sinfulness or imbibed the notion of the fear of God (Exodus 20:20). Their conception of God is dangerously over-familiar; perhaps he is merely the patron saint of their comfortable suburban lifestyle. For these people the depiction of a mirthful image of God may ultimately serve to reinforce already dangerous preconceptions.

---

3. Barbara Ehrenreich, *Bait and Switch: The (Futile) Pursuit of the American Dream* (New York: Henry Holt and Company, 2005), 139.

Rejecting Hierarchy in
God . . . and Beyond

The term "Job's comforter" has come down to us as a reference for someone who offers cold comfort in the midst of suffering. Rather than an empathetic shoulder to cry on, a Job's comforter offers a cool analysis of one's pain. Here we encounter an irony, for when God arrives on the scene he one-ups all of Job's "friends" by offering not a fatherly embrace, but rather a fierce blast of divine sovereignty, beginning with those piercing words: "Where were you when I laid the earth's foundation? Tell me, if you understand" (Job 38:4).

This picture of the fierce judge about summarizes the way that many people have viewed God. It is a picture of the unapproachable divine authority figure that comes to render judgment. And it finds little support within *The Shack*. In fact, rather than encourage conceptions of God as authoritarian while human beings are servile, *The Shack* encourages a picture of God submitting to us! Images of God laughing, joking, and even fumbling in the kitchen all serve to deconstruct the lofty images of deity that Christians have imbibed since their earliest days in front of the venerable Sunday school flannelgraph.

One would expect that shifting our view from the angry, haranguing deity of Job to the joking figure of *The Shack* would change how we view our relationship with God. And while the book clearly intends to do this, its intent is even more ambitious, for it challenges us to rethink (and reject) authoritarian structures wherever they are found. The assumption here is that if God comes to us not as authoritative judge but rather as humble servant, then we should adopt the servant's attitude of submission to one another. But to what extent? Apparently *The Shack* places no limit on this leveling of power and sees it as extending from marital and familial relations, through the church, and to the entire political and social organization of society. But ultimately it turns us back to God, for the spirit of submission that God expresses to creation is revealed to be part of God's own life. Contrary to the deep-seated assumption that God the Father is "in charge" of the Trinity, *The Shack* envisions the divine life as a community of mutual submission. Since the book's challenge to all conceptions of authority and submission begins here, this is where we shall begin as well.

Within *The Shack* the three divine persons are depicted as freely interacting with one another as intimate old friends. The picture is clearly intended to subvert any notion that the Son and Spirit submit to the Father. This image of perfect equality and mutual submission completely catches Mack off guard. Like so many Christians, he has always assumed the priority of the Father: "I know that you are all one and all, and that there are three of you. But you respond with such graciousness to each other. Isn't one of you more the boss than the other two?" (121). The question falls flat. Indeed, Papa, Jesus, and Sarayu respond with blank stares as if (though omniscient) they cannot even conceive of the notion of a hierarchy. But surely this cannot be right! It *must* be that Jesus and Sarayu are submitted to Papa. So Mack persists:

> "I am talking about who's in charge. Don't you have a chain of command?"

"Chain of command? That sounds ghastly!" Jesus said.

"At least binding," Papa added as they both started laughing, and then Papa turned to Mack and sang, "Though chains be of gold, they are chains all the same." (122)

Papa and Jesus could not be clearer. There simply is no room for submission to authority within God. Papa's words are particularly striking: chains of gold are still chains, and so is a chain of command!

One can appreciate Mack's perplexity. If a person has always assumed that within any social arrangement there must always be one individual in charge, then the rejection of a chain of authority could be very disconcerting, rather like getting in a car without a driver! So the question arises: if there is no top-down authority, then how is the divine life structured? Papa explains, "Mackenzie, we have no concept of final authority among us, only unity. We are in a *circle* of relationship, not a chain of command. . . . Hierarchy would make no sense among us" (122). Within the Trinity the entire notion of authority and submission makes no sense, for each person is submitted to the others. As Jesus explains, "That's the beauty you see in my relationship with Abba and Sarayu. We are indeed submitted to one another and have always been so and always will be. Papa is as much submitted to me as I to him, or Sarayu to me, or Papa to her. Submission is not about authority and it is not obedience; it is all about relationships of love and respect" (145).

From this perspective, the analogy of a driverless car careening madly down the street is simply misguided. A more apt analogy builds on the notion that authority is pointless in perfect community. As such, God is in no more need of a hierarchy of authority than the New Jerusalem will require a police service to enforce the rule of law! You don't need the police in a perfectly redeemed society. And you certainly don't need a captain for the good ship Trinity! The only time you might need to appeal to a person in charge is if there is a potential for conflict, and this certainly does not apply to God.

What exactly does this notion of mutual divine submission look like? Perhaps the single most vivid illustration comes when Mack witnesses a moment of devotional fellowship shared by Jesus and Papa. At the end of his first day with the Trinity, Mack watches Jesus take Papa's hands and lovingly share his appreciation for her submission: "I loved watching you today, as you made yourself fully available to take Mack's pain into yourself, and then give him space to choose his own timing. You honored him and you honored me" (107). Reading this passage one gets the sense that we, along with Mack, are allowed just a glimpse of the profound glory that Jesus shared with the Father before the world began (John 17:5). Could it really be that this exchange of mutual submission between Papa and Jesus captures the essence of God's glory?

If we accept that the Father, Son, and Spirit are mutually submitted to one another, we will find it affects a number of other theological views. Most immediately it will affect our understanding of how we relate to God. The common notion of divine/human relations is of God blasting down from on high while human beings grovel. Could it really be that the divine-human relationship is also characterized by mutual submission so that we are called to submit to God only because he has already submitted to us (145)? This is the conclusion that Mack comes to in the shack: " 'God, the servant,' he chuckled but then felt a welling up again as the thought made him pause. 'It is more truly God, my servant' " (236–237). God, my servant?! This is certainly a jolting phrase! How does one reconcile it with the idea that we are God's servants and he is the master? Think for instance of Jesus' chilling parable of God as the master who bequeathed gold to his servants to use for his gain. When he returns, he will judge the faithfulness of the servants, and the lazy servant will be cast out into the weeping and gnashing of teeth (Matthew 25:29). This doesn't sound like God is *our* servant!

Presumably the paradigm for God's servant relationship to us is found in Christ: though in very nature God, he did not consider equality with God something to hold on to, but instead emptied himself of his status, and *submitted* to the world in the form of a servant. Consider the profound words of the second century theologian Melito who observed, "you bound his good hands, which had formed you out of earth."[4] Did the hands that created all things really submit to being bound by human rebels? As incredible as this submission is, we need to emphasize as well that Christ did not become incarnate *despite* his divinity, as if he gave up his deity to become human, or perhaps was less fully divine to begin with. Rather, Jesus' actions truly are a revelation

---

4. Melito of Sardis, "A Homily on the Passover," in trans. and ed. Richard A. Norris, *The Christological Controversy* (Philadelphia: Fortress Press, 1980), 43.

of the servant heart of God. And if Jesus submitted to us, the Father too submitted to us by giving up his Son as they together work in one unified redemptive movement.

The idea that Father, Son, and Spirit submit to one another and to the world has all sorts of radical implications for human relations as well. To begin with, we are called to embody radical mutual submission at the heart of Christian discipleship. After all, we are called to take up our crosses which surely implies the willing surrender of any prerogatives of power (Luke 9:23; Ephesians 5:2; Philippians 2:5). Sadly, the temptation to find recourse to authority is great, for we *still* like to know that someone is in charge (especially if we're that person!). Who is going to call the meeting to order? Who can I go to if I have a complaint? Who is responsible for this mess? Where is the driver, manager, or head pastor? But this tendency to erect authority/submission hierarchies inevitably tends to marginalize the radical call for mutual submission. Take the example of marriage. Paul commands husband and wife to submit to one another (Ephesians 5:21). But rather than have this verse condition everything that follows, we have often focused on the very next verse as determinative: wives submit to your husbands (Ephesians 5:22)! When we insist on having somebody ultimately in charge we continue to perpetuate hierarchies that marginalize the call for mutual submission.

Interestingly, just as we like to know which persons carry the authority, so we often look to see which principles ought to be prioritized in our Christian walk. This can begin innocently enough, but if we are not careful it quickly devolves into a rigid legalism where following Christ is reduced to a list of dos and don'ts (206). But far from following a list of dos and don'ts, sanctification is about becoming a person who has been transformed into the image of Christ (Romans 8:29; 1 Corinthians 15:49; 2 Corinthians 3:18). Consequently, just as we reject ranking persons, so we need to reject ranking priorities. When Sarayu suggests as much to Mack, she is initially met by perplexity: "But don't you want us to set priorities? You know: God first, then whatever, followed by whatever?" (206). As tempting as such legalism may be, we need to recognize that the Christian life is not about following rules. Rather, it must always be centered on a relationship with Jesus (197).

The implications of *The Shack*'s anti-hierarchical thesis are even more radical when they are extended to the institutional, hierarchical church. The roots of the institutional church are deep indeed: one already sees authoritarian structures emerging within a couple decades of the Apostle John's death when Ignatius of Antioch famously instructed churches to "follow the bishop as Jesus Christ followed the Father."[5] From this humble beginning, the church has continued to develop complex institutions of authority and submission, frameworks which have tragically often led to coercive and oppressive abuses of authority which frustrate God's liberating intention for the church. One of the most shocking is surely the rampant sex abuse scandal among Catholic clergy: since 1950 the Catholic Church has paid out

---

5. Ignatius, "Epistle to the Smyrnaeans," in Henry Bettenson and Chris Maunder, *Documents of the Christian Church*, 3rd ed. (Oxford: Oxford University Press, 1999), 69.

over $2 billion dollars in settlements for sexual abuse claims.[6] One could certainly argue that the majority of these abuses were made possible because of a religious culture where the lowly laity were expected to be highly deferential to religious authorities. And this is ultimately rooted in a powerful authority/submission structure. Tragically, this structure has often given abusive priests free reign over the most vulnerable members of the church.

Still, it would surely be a mistake to blame one kind of church governance as if the problem was purely episcopal (the rule of bishops). Indeed, the dictatorial head pastor or board chair in a small Baptist church can wreak equally grievous abuses. And this turns us back to the radical nature of *The Shack*'s thesis: all such structures of authority and submission should be reconsidered. Mack too is deeply dissatisfied with the abuses in his own Christian background. But as Jesus explains, Mack's aversion to the church lies not with the church as God intended it. Rather, he is reacting understandably to the gradual accretion of abusive hierarchies of authority/submission. Thus Jesus seeks to soften Mack's aversion to the church by assuring him, "You're only seeing the institution, a man-made system. That's not what I came to build. What I see are people and their lives, a living breathing community of all those who love me, not buildings and programs" (178).

---

6. Meredith Buel, "Pope Expresses Deep Shame Over Clergy Sex Abuse Scandal," *Voice of America News* [online] available at http://www.voanews.com/english/archive/2008-04/2008-04-15-voa18.cfm?CFID=57282066&CFTOKEN=15404393.

The message is clear: if we are to recognize the true nature of the church, we should look not to the external, bureaucratic structures, but rather to people. Our problem is that the church, which consists of people in relation to God and each other, has often been obscured by its all-too-fallible visible institutions. And so the key to liberating the church is found in recognizing that its life is rooted not in institutions, but rather in the love and mutual submission modeled by Papa, Jesus, and Sarayu.

We need to appreciate how radical this non-institutional conception of the church really is. According to Jesus, the church consists in "relationships and simply sharing life" (178). What is striking is what this minimalistic definition of church excludes: it says nothing about the nature or administration of sacraments, the ordination of clergy, the organization or mission of the church, the commissioning of art and architecture, the formulation and refinement of creeds and catechisms, the exercise of church discipline, the place of social and political action, and much more. Indeed, Jesus' minimalistic definition implies that God would look askance upon all such questions of institutional formation, preferring instead that we focus all our energy upon the cultivation of individual relationships. In fact, it would seem that the optimal Christian community looks very much like the thousands of house churches that now dot the suburbs of North America: perhaps a dozen believers sharing the Word and song in someone's humble living room. All this suggests that Jesus might have a few things to say to the pope. If Jesus' words to Mack are any guide, he would probably instruct the pontiff to sell off all the church's property, dispense with the bishops and bureaucracy, donate his papal tiara and vestments to the local Goodwill, and join a house church!

This repudiation of any organizing principles or hierarchies of power also extends to the organization of all of society: "'I'm not too big on religion,' Jesus said a little sarcastically, 'and not very fond of politics or economics either.' Jesus' visage darkened noticeably. 'And why should I be? They are the man-created trinity of terrors that ravages the earth'" (179). With these strong words, the rejection of institutional hierarchies is extended to every dimension of society. Thus in *The Shack* Jesus criticizes all hierarchies, including those that structure human institutions from the state to marriage, as requiring laws and enforcement of laws which lead to oppression and inhibit the development of true relationship (122–123).

Rethinking Hierarchy in the World

The Shack certainly must be given credit for presenting an ambitious and far-reaching thesis. But to what extent should (or can) we reject all hierarchies? Rather than address each one of the areas raised in the book, I'll focus on the prioritization of rules within the Christian life, the organization of the church, and the organization of society.

The question "How does one become like Christ?" is a Christian version of a more general question: "How does one become a good person?" This question has preoccupied thinkers for centuries. Many of those who have thought about ethical formation have found it tempting to find recourse to rules, as if one could be ethical simply by following the right rules. But a purely rule-based approach to ethics or sanctification is reductionistic and legalistic. Yet can we therefore conclude that rules and the prioritization of rules have no place in the life of discipleship? After all, when Jesus was asked about priorities, he identified *two* priorities: "Love the Lord your God with all your heart and with all your soul and with all your mind" (Matthew 22:37) and " 'Love your neighbor as yourself.' All the Law and the Prophets hang on these two commandments" (Matthew 22:39–40). So it would seem that we cannot simply talk about the journey to holiness as a relationship with Jesus, for that journey is directed by these two principles.

What about *The Shack*'s view of the organized church? Here I think we need to be especially careful given that the book's conception of church is not that revolutionary after all; indeed, it looks strikingly like a typical "low church Protestantism." As George Marsden has observed, "One of the striking features of much of evangelicalism is its general disregard for the in-stitutional church."[7] Like other rejections of the institutional church, one finds here both trenchant critiques as well as overly simplistic solutions. Surely it is correct to say that the church is a people in special relationship with God, each other, and the world. But this does not require us to marginalize the institu-tional expression of the church. Is it not possible that the same God who speaks through spontaneous charismatic experiences and intimate communal gatherings in one's living room, might also work through the beauty of the Anglican Book of Common

---

7. Cited in Stanley J. Grenz, *Renewing the Center: Evangelical Theology in a Post-Theological Era* (Grand Rapids, MI: Baker Academic, 2000), 288.

Prayer, the mystical Eastern Orthodox liturgy, and even the austere Roman Catholic College of Cardinals (along with the Pope!)? Might it be that a categorical rejection of institutional hierarchy represents an overreaction to the abuse of power in favor of a rather naïve assumption that "all you need is love"?

Our questions continue when we turn to consider hierarchy with the secular state. After all, Paul appears to affirm the state as a God-ordained power: "Let everyone be subject to the governing authorities, for there is no authority except that which God has established. The authorities that exist have been established by God" (Romans 13:1). And it certainly is no secret that Paul made good use of the authority and status that he derived from his Roman citizenship (see Acts 16:37; 22:25,28). Indeed, the sweeping condemnation of authority/submission hierarchies in *The Shack* leaves it unclear whether it is permissible for Christians to serve in the police or military, or in judicial, legislative, or executive branches of government. (If all such participation is denied, then *The Shack* faces the same counter-cultural weaknesses as classic Anabaptism.) More radically, it leaves one wondering whether there ought to be even secular governance or whether the book in fact espouses anarchy (literally: no rule)!

Any attempt to move beyond authority/submission structures faces one huge problem: we don't live in a perfect world. Children still need to be corrected by parents, police need to reign in civil disobedience, and entire armies may even be required to restore the rule of law. Practically speaking how does *The Shack* propose we live in this world? Importantly, the book leaves open the possibility of participating in these fallen structures. As Papa observes, "We work within your systems even while we seek to free you from them" (123). As such, it may be that Papa would advocate Christians continue to participate within the authority/submission structures that dominate the political, economic, and social landscape. However, if such participation is allowed it is not without obligation; rather, Christians should participate within fallen structures of power with the intent and goal of redeeming them to the point where the hierarchy of power no longer remains. To say the least, if this view were followed consistently, it would turn Christianity into a radical agent for social and political change.

The Son Will Be Made Subject to Him

While Papa, Jesus, and Sarayu all speak unambiguously against any form of authority/submission in healthy relationships, it must be said that the actual witness of Scripture is much more ambiguous. Indeed, one could derive a scriptural basis for hierarchy within the Trinity beginning with Philippians 2. Here we need to keep in mind the importance for theologians of what I call the "God is as God reveals" principle. According to this principle, theology depends upon the assumption that the way God reveals himself in the world is a faithful reflection of the way God really is. For example, if God reveals himself to be a loving community of three distinct persons, then he actually is a loving community of three distinct persons. We don't speculate that God really might be four or five persons, or one person playing three roles. This principle is crucial, because if we didn't accept it, we would lose any ability to know anything of God in himself.

Let's keep the God is as God reveals principle in mind as we turn back to Philippians 2. Here we face an important question: why was it the Son who made himself nothing, and the Father who then exalted the Son? According to our principle it is reasonable to infer that this pattern of God's action in history is not arbitrary, but rather that it reflects something about the eternal relations in the Trinity. In the same way that the revelation of God as three persons leads us to conclude that God really is three persons, so the revelation of the Father/Son relation as authority/submission leads us to conclude that the Father/Son relation is authority/submission.

Indeed, if we pull back to consider the entire sweep of the New Testament we find this pattern is more widely represented. The Father sends both Christ (John 5:26; 6:57; 1 John 4:14) and the Spirit (John 14:26; Galatians 4:6) into the world. In turn, the Son reflects a submission to the Father's will throughout his life (Matthew 26:39; Galatians 1:4). He tells his disciples that he speaks by the Father's authority (John 14:10) and does exactly what the Father commands: "For I did not speak on my own, but the Father who sent me commanded me to say all that I have spoken" (John 12:49; 14:31). And so while Jesus certainly did not wish to face the suffering of the cross, he nonetheless submitted to the will of his Father: "My Father, if it is possible, may this cup be taken from me. Yet not as I will, but as you will" (Matthew 26:39).

To go further, we could conclude that there *is* something like a chain of command in God. If the Son appears to be submitted to the Father, the Spirit in turn appears to be submitted to the Son. Consider that the Spirit is sent by the Son to the disciples, and will only speak what he hears (John 16:13) to the end of glorifying the Son (John 16:14). In addition, while one finds both the Father and Son being worshipped in Scripture (Revelation 5:11–13), one does not find equivalent places where worship is directed to the Spirit. We should not conclude from this that the Spirit is not divine or worthy of worship. Rather it points us back to the Spirit's specific role being concerned with the exaltation of the Son. And ultimately the work of both Jesus and the Spirit is directed back to the Father (Romans 15:6; Ephesians 3:20–21). Although there are a few places where Jesus refers to the Father glorifying him (John 8:54; 17:5) in a way that seems to reverse the order, even this occurs so that Christ might glorify the Father (John 17:1). As such, one could legitimately conclude that God consists of a hierarchy running upwards from the Spirit through the Son and ultimately to the Father.

When one considers this set of texts in light of the "God is as God reveals" principle, we have very strong grounds to conclude that there is an authority/submission hierarchy within the Trinity. However, things are not quite that simple, for if we are not careful the principle could end up proving too much. After all, when Jesus was called "Good teacher" he replied, "No one is good—except God alone" (Luke 18:19). In addition, Jesus observed that "the Father is greater than I" (John 14:28) and noted concerning his return that only the Father knows the day or hour (Matthew 24:36). The danger then is that a "God is as God reveals" reading of these texts may force us to say that the Son is less than the Father!

Since orthodox Christians are unwilling to accept that conclusion, they have typically dealt with these difficult inferiority texts by limiting their application to Christ's humble state in the incarnation in which he emptied himself of his divine status (Philippians 2:7). That is, Jesus is not lesser than the Father *except* in the limitations of the incarnation. And while he is omniscient in his divinity, as a human he did not know the day or hour of his return. But if we can marginalize these inferiority texts this easily, why not extend the same treatment to the Christ and Spirit submission texts? Hence, we could say that the Son and Spirit assumed a submission to the Father only in the world while it could just as well have been the Father who adopted the submissive role. *The Shack* seems to say something more radical yet. While it is true that the Son and Spirit submitted to the Father, in doing so they were not merely stepping down from the glory of divinity for a time, but rather were expressing the very nature of God. True leadership is found in the one who submits: "For who is greater, the one who is at the table or the one who serves?" (Luke 22:27). As such, in coming into the world to serve humanity, the Son and Spirit were expressing the glory of God no less than the Father.

At this point we seem to be at something of an impasse. It appears that, depending on one's assumptions, one can read the New Testament to support either the Father's authority or the mutual submission of the three. But perhaps there is another way to establish whether hierarchy exists in God: to identify texts which depict authority/submission relations continuing after the completion of the redemptive roles that Christ and the Spirit assume within creation.

To begin with, we could note the significance of Romans 11:36 in which Paul says that all things are from, through and to God the Father. This verse appears to move beyond God's action in history to assert the Father's priority in eternity. So, the consummation of reconciliation is always depicted as occurring through Christ back to God the Father (Colossians 1:20). In keeping with our observation that God's exaltation of the Son brings glory back to himself, Paul declares that "every tongue acknowledge that Jesus Christ is Lord, to the glory of God the Father" (Philippians 2:11). Taken together, such passages seem to point toward the continued authority and priority of the Father in eternity. But the most significant passage is found in 1 Corinthians 15:24–28:

> Then the end will come, when he hands over the kingdom to God the Father after he has destroyed all dominion, authority and power. For he must reign until he has put all his enemies under his feet. The last enemy to be destroyed is death. For he "has put everything under his feet." Now when it says that "everything" has been put under him, it is clear that this does not include God himself, who put everything under Christ. When he has done this, then the Son himself will be made subject to him who put everything under him, so that God may be all in all.

In this passage Paul moves beyond Christ's action in redemptive history to the backdrop of eternity. Thus when reconciliation is complete, Christ will hand the kingdom back to the Father. This passage would certainly seem to imply (if not explicitly teach) the continued submission of the Son under the Father's perfect authority.

The questions of authority and submission in God and the world are great and cannot be settled here. But having ventured into the midst of the discussion, one could get the feeling that there may be more common ground than is commonly recognized. If the Trinity is a perfect community of three persons, what sense is there in appeals to the Father's authority over the Son and Spirit? And to the extent that we attempt to justify our appeals to authority and power by pointing to the Father's authority over the Son we miss the point, for the Father would never *impose* authority, as we are often wont to do.

We may inevitably find ourselves participating in structures of power in this world, but what if those who found themselves in leadership positions assumed the true role of a servant leader? Not that trite cliché of the business leadership literature, a leader who gives up his parking space and privileges to motivate productivity and build morale. Instead, what about true servant leadership expressed in Christ's service to us? What if presidents, pastors and husbands/fathers expressed whatever God-given authority they might have by keeping the feet of those under their authority sparklingly clean (John 13:14–16)?

I suspect that then we might find ourselves moving beyond the authority/submission debate altogether.

DIGGING DEEPER

(1) How do you react to the depiction of God in *The Shack* as mirthful and laughing?

(2) Do you believe that hierarchies of power in marriage, the church, and/or the wider society need to be rejected or that they should be reformed? If the latter, what would truly reformed hierarchies look like?

(3) Do you believe that authority/submission exists within the Trinity? If so, how would you respond to the argument that if Christ is eternally subordinate then he is inferior?

(4) Do you agree that the essence of church is found in personal relationship? What implications does that view have for the traditional institutional structures, offices, practices, and missions of the church?

(5) Jesus undoubtedly assumed the role of a servant. But is he our servant now?

CHAPTER 5

THE BIGGEST PROBLEM IN THE UNIVERSE

It is his moment of truth. Mack is in the cave being interrogated by the mysterious female figure that he would later learn is Sophia. To this point he has been suppressing the fact that he still blames God for the loss of Missy. (Apparently Mack has not yet come to terms with the futility of trying to hide his true feelings from the God that knows everything.) Determined to get Mack to admit to his anger against God, Sophia pointedly asks: "Isn't that your complaint, Mackenzie? That God has failed you, that he failed Missy? That before the Creation, God knew that one day your Missy would be brutalized, and still he created? And then he *allowed* that twisted soul to snatch her from your loving arms when he had the power to stop him. Isn't God to blame, Mackenzie?" (161). Sophia will not stop until she gets an honest answer. As she persists, Mack's defenses begin to break down until all his pent up anger finally bubbles to the surface and he responds with fury: *Yes! God is to blame!!* He is to blame for the hurricane that floods a coastal city! He is to blame for the refugees slaughtered in the midst of a bloody war! He is to blame for the young man dying of cancer! And he is most surely to blame for the death of an innocent little child at the hands of a sadistic maniac! What could possibly be said in the defense of a God who not only anticipated, but even planned for and oversaw each of these horrors?

How Could God Be Especially Fond of Missy?

Soon after Mack meets Papa, she begins to mention all the people of whom she is especially fond. The list continues to grow until Mack finally realizes that her fondness is in fact without limit: "When I think of each of my children individually, I find that I am especially fond of each one" (155; see also 118–119). But if God is especially fond of everybody, why does the world not reflect that fact? Why is it that so often God seems arbitrary and capricious? Alas, examples are not hard to find.

Just consider the case at the heart of *The Shack*. At the same time that Missy disappears, young Amber Ducette from the neighboring campsite also turns up missing. Initially everyone hopes that Missy and Amber will be found together. Nonetheless, Amber's father Emil is clearly relieved when he returns to the camp shortly thereafter to report that his daughter was discovered safe: "'We found her,' explained Emil, his face lighting up, then turning somber as he realized what he had implied. 'I mean, we found Amber'" (45). Even as Emil's fear dissolved into relief, Mack's would continue to build until it would culminate in the horrifying realization that Missy had been abducted by a serial killer. But how could this have happened? If God is especially fond of Missy (92, 167, 185) and her father (92, 234), then how could he have allowed her to become the star attraction in the nightmarish fantasies of a sociopathic pervert?

If only the horror of *The Shack* were a one-off anomaly. But, tragically, this disparity of outcomes is repeated countless times around the world every day in a myriad of ways. It is seen when one man's house is destroyed by a tornado while his neighbor's remains untouched, or when one woman lives into her nineties while her twin sister died of cholera as an infant. Too often the same providence that offers a warm pat to one person strikes out with a backhand to another. The point was memorably made by nineteenth century atheist Robert Ingersoll who described one man's description of God's providential hand on his life: "A few years ago he was about to go on a ship, when he was detained. He did not go, and the ship was lost with all on board. 'Yes!' I said, 'do you think the people who were drowned believed in special Providence?'"[1] Ingersoll's disgust is understandable. Too often those who find themselves benefitting from the warm pat of providence overlook the agony of those who receive the stinging backhand.

So why is it that some people are subjected to incredible agonies throughout their lives while others enjoy all the pleasures this world can offer? Surely this widespread disparity cannot be due to human merit (as if we always got just what we deserved), for many scoundrels have enjoyed the warm pat of providence while many saints have suffered the stinging backhand (think Job). But then if providential blessings and pains do not reflect our worthiness, is God just cruelly arbitrary, like the sociopathic Mafioso who can coolly murder an associate at lunch and then bounce his toddler on his knee before dinner?

Stated as such the objection presumes that God is behind every event, planning each one. But why think that God exercises this kind of control? Maybe this is where the problem arises. Rather than thinking of God as a micromanager overseeing every detail, wouldn't it be better to think of him as a CEO who runs a vast Fortune 500 company? The CEO's role is not to manage paper clip supplies, but rather to run the multinational empire. So, by the same token, isn't it better to think of God as running a vast creation while not concerning himself directly with the details?

There is no doubt that the God of "big picture providence" who cannot bother with the details is a tempting option. It

---

1. Robert G. Ingersoll, *Lectures and Essays, (The Three Series in One Volume)* (London: Watts & Co., 1926), second series, 117.

sounds appropriately lordly and yet does not directly implicate God in specific instances of evil and suffering. Unfortunately, it contradicts the biblical view that God's meticulous concern for creation extends down to the number of hairs on our heads (Matthew 10:30) and out to all events as God "works out everything in conformity with the purpose of his will" (Ephesians 1:11). Given passages like this, it is hardly surprising that the mainstream theological position has always viewed God's providence as meticulous (covering every detail). A particularly lucid and intriguing presentation of the traditional perspective is found in *Lake Wobegon Days*, Garrison Keillor's fictional account of small town life. At one point Keillor narrates a debate among the young boys of the town concerning God's foreknowledge and providence:

> Near the clearing was a giant tree we called the Pee Tree; a long rope hung from a lower branch, which when you swung hard on it took you out over the edge and showed you your real death. You could let go at the end of the arc and fall to the rocks and die if you wanted to.
>
> Jim said, "It's not that far—it wouldn't kill you." He was bucking for captain. Lance said, "So jump then. I dare you." That settled it. It would kill you, all right. It would break every bone in your body, just like Richard. He was twelve and drove his dad's tractor and fell off and it ran over him and killed him. He was one boy who died when I was a boy, and the other was Paulie who drowned in the lake. Both were now in heaven

with God where they were happy. It was God's will that it would happen. [2]

> God created the world and ordained everything to be right and perfect, then man sinned against God's Will, but God still knew *everything*. Before the world was made, when it was only darkness and mist and waters, God was well aware of Lake Wobegon, my family, our house, and He had me all sketched out down to what size my feet would be (big), which bike I would ride (a Schwinn), and the five ears of corn I'd eat for supper that night.[3]

This is surprisingly sophisticated theology for young boys! According to the Christian tradition it is indeed correct to say that God foreknew (and in some sense willed) the size of our feet, the type of bike we ride, and even the menu for every meal of our lives (Psalm 139:16), even as God controls the whole sweep of cosmic history. There is nothing too magnificent or miniscule to escape God's meticulous providential control.

Unfortunately, the degree to which the Christian affirms meticulous providential control is precisely the degree to which one is forced to confront the problem of evil. When discussing the problem of evil it has often been tempting to abstract the discussion to a generalized notion of "evil," which is kept at a safe distance from real, concrete cases. (Evil as an abstract

---

2. Garrison Keillor, *Lake Wobegon Days* (New York: Penguin, 1986), 11.
3. Keillor, *Lake Wobegon Days*, 12.

category lacks emotional bite.) Yet if God knows such trivialities as how much corn we will eat for dinner, then he knew that
Richard would be killed by a tractor and Paulie would drown
in the lake. So why did he allow these horrific events? And why
did he allow that murder that sits like a black hole at the center
of *The Shack*? Surely on this point we all agree with Mack:
"Even in such a world of relative morality, causing harm to a
child is still considered absolutely wrong. Period!" (59). Nor
are we simply speaking in the present case only of harming a
child, but of (presumably) raping and then murdering her! So
how do we reconcile the goodness of God with the incredible
evil of Missy's death?

We can present the dilemma between God's providential
control and goodness and the existence of evil as follows:

(1) As all-loving, God would want to prevent every evil.

(2) As all-powerful, God could prevent every evil.

(3) Missy was murdered by a serial killer.

Surely if God is all-loving he would not have desired that Missy
be murdered by a serial killer. If love means *anything* it means
that God would spare a sweet, innocent child from the horrors
that Missy experienced! As Jesus put it, "If you, then, though
you are evil, know how to give good gifts to your children, how
much more will your Father in heaven give good gifts to those
who ask him!" (Matthew 7:11). And surely if God is all-powerful
he could have prevented Missy from being murdered by a serial
killer. After all, "Is anything too hard for the LORD?" (Genesis

18:14; see also Jeremiah 32:27). So how can we reconcile God as all-loving and all-powerful to Missy's death?

The attempt to explain how the goodness and love of God can be reconciled with the problem of evil is called theodicy. According to the classic definition coined by John Milton, a theodicy seeks "to justify the ways of God to man." That is, it seeks to explain how the existence of evil is compatible with God's perfect nature. We will begin with two straightforward ways that one might reconcile God's existence with Missy's tragic death: either deny that God is all-loving or deny that he is all-powerful.

Rethinking God's Love

Our first pass at theodicy will consider the possibility that God is not all-loving. While this may come as a surprise to many Christians, this is the position of a major theological tradition called Calvinism (named after its most influential exponent John Calvin). To be more specific, Calvinists believe that God is perfect in his love, but he chooses not to show this love to all his creatures.

To begin with, the Calvinist believes that God controls all events perfectly, including free human choices. That is, God gives us the desires that we freely fulfill, both good and bad. (Other Christians disagree and think instead that while God can know what we will do in advance, he cannot make us do it if we are truly free.) As a result, Calvinists believe that God could have made the world such that Adam and Eve would never have fallen. It follows that Adam and Eve sinned because God gave them the free desires to sin. Likewise, the Little Ladykiller sinned because God gave him the will to sin. Everyone who sins does so because God has formed his or her character to do so. As Paul tersely put it, "Therefore God has mercy on whom he wants to have mercy, and he hardens whom he wants to harden" (Romans 9:18). So the reason there is evil in the world is simple: though perfectly loving, God wants there to be some evil!

This Calvinist view raises an obvious question: why would a perfectly loving God desire evil in the world? In order to explain this, the Calvinist denies what many Christians assume: that God loves all his creatures equally. Rather, God's ultimate concern is to manifest his glory most fully. Therefore, God is concerned to ensure that creation provides the best opportunity for God to display his magnificent attributes. Consider this analogy: if we think of the great political leaders of history we will find that the leaders most revered are those who led their people through times of great adversity. Think of Winston Churchill barking out defiantly against the Führer his famous "We shall fight them on the beaches" speech. It was the adversity of wartime that allowed Churchill's stellar leadership qualities to emerge. Similarly, adversity within creation provides an opportunity for God to display his leadership qualities.

In the midst of adversity God is able to manifest his mercy and love to those creatures he has decreed to choose the good. At the same time, he manifests his wrath and justice to those creatures he has decreed to choose the evil (Romans 9:22–23). Through all the good and evil, God's glory is more fully on display than if he had willed a creation where everyone did his will perfectly. One final point: the same reasoning that applies to the present age applies in eternity as well. There, too, rebellion must be present so God's fullest display of attributes can be manifest. As such, Calvinists believe that God decrees that some people would reject the offer of salvation so that God can rightly damn them eternally and thereby ensure that his perfect wrath and justice are both forever on display.

Calvinism has biblical texts to which it can appeal in support. For instance, the Israelites ultimately went to war against Canaan to display God's power and wrath: "For it was the LORD himself who hardened their hearts to wage war against Israel, so that he might destroy them totally, exterminating them without mercy, as the LORD had commanded" (Joshua 11:20). Just as God hardened the hearts of the Canaanites so that he might judge them for their wickedness, might God have hardened the heart of Missy's killer so he might judge him? "It was the LORD himself who hardened the Little Ladykiller's heart to kill Missy." If so, then we could explain Missy's death as one way that God displays his glory more fully, perhaps by exercising his wrath and justice in the temporal (or eternal) punishment of the killer.

I confess that I am one of many people who find Calvinism not only unpalatable but nearly incomprehensible. Let's start with God's glory. I don't accept that the only way to have a high appreciation of God's glory is by seeing God crush human rebellion. There have been many great leaders in history who have led their people in peacetime. Couldn't God have fully displayed his attributes through peaceful rule as well? Indeed, Calvinism is in danger of Manichaeism, the view that good and evil are equal and necessary opposites so that good can only be known to the extent that evil exists. But my biggest problem is with Calvinism's view of God's love. Contrary to the Calvinist claim that God only loves some creatures and hates others, I believe that God loves all people (1 Timothy 2:4; 2 Peter 3:9). *The Shack* believes this as well since Papa is adamant that she is especially fond of *all* her creatures. In fact, when Mack comes to the cabin he appears to hold a Calvinist view, for he assumes that God chooses to save some people and damn others. Indeed, it is this assumption which haunts Mack by making God seem cruel and arbitrary. But Sophia is determined to challenge this assumption. To illustrate how misguided his thinking is, she forces him to be honest about his own accusation against God. To this end, she demands that he choose which of his children will be damned eternally. When Mack recoils in horror at the very thought, Sophia calmly replies: "I am only asking you to do something that you believe God does" (162). The book implies that God is even more horrified than Mack at the suggestion that the divine love might be limited. And so this first attempt at theodicy is not open to us.

Rethinking God's Power

If we refuse to accept any limitation in God's love for creation, we could still resolve the problem of evil by accepting a limit to his power. In other words, God is not able to prevent or eliminate all evil. This is the way that Rabbi Harold Kushner explained the goodness of God after his three year old son Aaron was diagnosed with progeria, a terrible disease in which the afflicted child ages at an accelerated rate until he/she dies of old age, typically in the early teen years. (Aaron died when he was fourteen.) As Kushner bluntly put it, "God does not want you to be sick or crippled. He didn't make you have this problem, and He doesn't want you to go on having it, but He can't make it go away. That is something which is too hard even for God."[4] According to Kushner, when suffering happens to us it is not for us to ask why it happened because *there is no reason*. Sometimes evil happens, but God is doing his best to fight it.

Kushner's views of God as limited (even impotent) never caught on with evangelicals. However, a modified limitation view has recently attracted much interest from some evangelicals. According to this view, known as Open Theism, God wanted free creatures to populate his world. And creatures can only be free if God does not know what they will do. To explain, consider this illustration: if God foreknew that I would eat a bowl of pasta for lunch tomorrow then it would seem I could not choose to eat anything else but that bowl of pasta. If God knows I *will* do it, then I *must* do it. But since God wants me to be free in my choices, including my lunch choices, then he cannot know what I will choose. As a result, it must be that God will learn tomorrow what I will choose to eat along with the rest of us. I *might* eat pasta, I *might* eat a hot dog, and then again I *might* just skip a meal. God will just have to wait and see.

Open theists believe that they are being faithful to the biblical depictions of God learning, changing his mind, and failing

---

4. Harold S. Kushner, *When Bad Things Happen to Good People* (New York: Avon Books, 1981), 129.

to anticipate eventual outcomes. They complain that Christians have been too quick to "dismiss" these texts as anthropomorphisms (as we did in chapter two). Like us, God faces the future as an unknown. Indeed, God may find himself saying "Whoa, I didn't see that coming!" (Genesis 6:6–7). But even if this happens, we need not worry too much: God is infinitely resourceful to face whatever comes to be, so that ultimately he will see his plans accomplished.

Again, even as infinitely resourceful, God cannot prevent every evil situation that arises. Even if success in the war is secured, there may be many unexpected casualties in the battle. This means that the open theist takes a view of God's relation to evil that is similar to Kushner: the open theist affirms that God is unable to prevent every evil and that there are many horrible events that simply have *no point*. That is, there are many events that God didn't know would happen, and that he didn't want to happen, but now that they have happened, he will do his best to bring good out of them.

So it may be with Missy's death. There is no reason why this happened; God did not foresee it, and when it happened, it shocked and saddened God as much as Mack. But God will work to bring good out of it.

Just as *The Shack* shuts the door to Calvinism, so it blocks off the way to Open Theism. The strongest statement comes when Papa explains to Mack her unique perspective on the repeated mistakes made by fallen human beings:

> "Let's say, for example, I am trying to teach you how not
> to hide inside of lies, hypothetically of course," she said

with a wink. "And let's say that I know it will take you forty-seven situations and events before you will actually hear me—that is, before you will hear clearly enough to agree with me and change. So when you don't hear me the first time, I'm not frustrated or disappointed, I'm thrilled. Only forty-six more times to go." (187)

Since Open Theism claims that God cannot know even one future free human action, this statement contradicts Open Theism forty-seven times! And I believe *The Shack* is right to do so, for Scripture repeatedly affirms that God foreknows all events, including human actions (see for instance Isaiah 46:10; Luke 22:34, 60; Acts 4:28; 1 Peter 1:1–2). This view has significant implications for it implies that *nothing is left to chance in God's world*. As John Calvin observed, "I see that men have a very bad custom, that where one ought to say 'God willed this,' they say 'fortune willed this.'"[5] We cannot explain Missy's death simply as bad luck. As Papa explains, everything is part of the divine plan:

> "Mack," said Papa with an intensity that caused him to listen very carefully, "we want to share with you the love and joy and freedom and light that we already know within ourself. We created you, the human, to be in face-to-face relationship with us, to join our circle of love. As difficult as it will be for you to understand, *everything that has taken place is occurring exactly*

---

5. John Calvin, *Institutes of the Christian Religion*, vol. 1, ed. John T. McNeill, trans. Ford Lewis Battles (London: SCM Press, 1961), 208.

according to this purpose, without violating choice or will" (124–125, emphasis added).

Troubling thought it may be to admit, Missy's murder was part of God's purpose or plan.

Before we pursue this claim further, we should also point out that Open Theism does not absolve God of responsibility in Missy's death. According to the FBI, the Little Ladykiller probably spent a full day or two stalking Missy (57). Even if God did not know the killer's exact next move, God *certainly* was aware of his intentions. After all, he had seen him do it before! And yet God never intervened to stop the murder, even though he could have done it in innumerable ways without violating anyone's free will. For instance, he could have strategically placed a tree branch on the path that would cause the killer to fall and sprain his ankle. Or perhaps at the moment that the killer was closing in on Missy sitting at the picnic table, God could have ensured that a meteorite would hurtle out of the sky leaving a smoking crater where the killer once stood. (Incidentally, that's my favorite outcome as it is very close to a good old fashioned divine smiting!) Perhaps after Missy had been abducted, God could have placed a nail on the road which would puncture the Little Ladykiller's tire, making escape impossible. But instead of preventing the crime in one of these ways, God allowed it to unfold over several agonizing hours. Can we really say that God didn't see this coming, or that he allowed it to happen for no reason?

God in Search of Greater Goods

If we agree with *The Shack* that evil cannot be explained because of a limit in God's love or his power, then why does he allow evil? Let's begin with an analogy. Little Jamie is having a wonderful day playing at home when suddenly her mom interrupts her play to take her to the doctor. Jamie replies that she is not sick, but her mom insists. When they arrive at the clinic, Jamie is ushered into a room and a nurse comes in with a long, scary needle. As Jamie is instructed to name all the Sesame Street characters on the wall poster, the child suddenly feels the pain of this needle plunging into her arm. Shortly thereafter Jamie begins to feel unwell and she develops a slight fever that evening. Although she feels better the next day, she cannot understand why, when she was perfectly healthy, her mother would make her have a painful and scary needle that would make her sick.

While this may be a problem for Jamie, *we* can know that her mother was seeing to it that Jamie received a flu shot to prevent her from contracting a potentially fatal illness. In fact we can think of many cases where children are subjected to pain because their parents have a greater purpose that the children cannot understand. Could it be that God too has reasons sufficient to justify incredible evils like Missy's murder? And might we reconcile God's perfect love and power with evil in this way? This idea is known as a *greater goods* theodicy, and the basic idea is that God allows particular evils to occur because he intends to draw greater goods out of them. But what kind of goods would God plan to bring out of creation? Let's consider two: free will and moral development or soul-making.

According to the Calvinist view, free will consists of a person being able to do whatever God has made them desire to do. But many people find that idea to make no sense. Surely if I am truly free then not even God can decide my will: I must make my own decisions. And that means that if I am free I must be able to choose good or evil. As such, God creates free creatures because it is a moral good, even though he knows that it will result in a limited amount of evil.

Consider the Tiny Tykes piano. This is a toddler's piano with a measly four keys on the keyboard: C, E, G, and high C. This limited selection of keys has an important by-product: the sounding of any combination of these keys always produces a harmonious sound; it is simply impossible to produce dissonance or cacophony on this piano. But consider what is lost! With such a limited set of keys we cannot even play "Rock-a-Bye-Baby," let alone Rachmaninoff! As such, anyone who is seriously interested in teaching their child piano will instead opt for a keyboard with all 88 keys. Although they recognize that this will result in some frustration given the potential for dissonance, it is more than offset by the potential for much more complex music.

By the same token, God could have created creatures that could not choose evil. But instead he created free creatures with the potential for evil, recognizing that ultimately the good of truly free creatures would more than offset the limited dissonance. The idea that free will is a greater good is central to *The Shack*'s theodicy (125). Papa explains that "All evil flows from independence, and independence is your choice. If I were to simply revoke all the choices of independence, the world as you know it would cease to exist and love would have no meaning" (190). In other words for love to be meaningful it requires freedom. Again, Papa warns: "If I were to simply revoke all the choices of independence, the world as you know it would cease to exist and love would have no meaning. This world is not a playground where I keep all my children free from evil. Evil is the chaos of this age that you brought to me, but it will not have the final say" (94–95). Love is not meaningful if it is compelled and determined. Only if it is freely chosen is it significant. Thus, the evil of the world arises from the choices of human beings which God allows because of his desire to be in relation with truly free creatures.

The goods for which God allows evil also extend to the processes by which people come to make better choices, and this brings us to the idea of moral development or soul-making. Just as a rigorous exercise program of body-making will involve much physical pain, so the process of soul-making, of becoming a more responsible moral person in the image of Christ, will entail some physical and emotional pain. In order to develop a solid moral character one must experience some frustration, disappointment, danger, and scarcity of resources. Only then will one learn to be patient, hopeful, courageous, and generous.

To illustrate, within Roald Dahl's book *Charlie and the Chocolate Factory* there is a horrid little girl named Veruca Salt who gets whatever she wants. When Veruca wants to win one of the golden tickets to visit Mr. Wonka's factory, her father shuts down his entire nut factory and instructs all his employees to spend their days unwrapping Wonka bars! Veruca is absolutely intolerable until a few days later when she gets her ticket. Absolutely unable to handle any denial of her demands, she is a self-centered, spoiled brat. Imagine if Veruca's parents had disciplined her properly and taught her virtues of patience, self-denial, and generosity. She would not only be a much better child, but a happier one as well. (But alas, then she would have been a much duller character in the book!)

And so, God allows us to experience suffering and evil to spur on our moral development (Proverbs 3:11–12; Hebrews 12:5–6) to the end that we will be able to enter the divine circle of Love. This dimension of the greater goods theodicy is implied in the book when Papa promises to Mack, "If you could only see how all of this ends and what we will achieve without the violation of one human will—then you would understand" (125). Not only is God respecting human will, but he is drawing those free creatures on to maturity through the occasionally painful process of soul-making. Could we begin to speculate on which character-forming goods God might have drawn out of Missy's death? It is certainly possible that Missy could have developed bravery and trust in God through the ordeal. Mack's transformation is more obvious, for he moves from being harshly judgmental of God and the human race to being one who lives in humility and love. The transformation is evident when we contrast Mack's initial desire that Missy's killer be damned to hell (161) with his later desire to extend forgiveness to the killer (248). Could it be that Mack's transformation provides one piece in the explanation of Missy's death?

Are We Mere Means to God's Ends?

According to the greater goods theodicy, God allows everything bad that happens for a greater good. God allowed Mack to slip and fall on his driveway in the ice storm because of the greater goods that God sought to bring out of this event. The same is true of the time when, as a child, Mack was tied to a tree and beaten by his father for two days. Even in the case of Missy being murdered by a sociopath, God purposes the event to draw out greater goods. Such is the power of this explanation that it neatly explains every horrific evil with the promise that each contributes to a total greater good than would have otherwise come about had the event not occurred.

Still, while the greater goods theodicy may be plausible as a general explanation of evil, it immediately begins to run into a problem when we seek to apply it to specific cases like Missy's murder. To put it bluntly, there is something deeply unsatisfying about explaining such a horrendous evil as part of God's "magnificent tapestry" (176). Does this not make God look shockingly calloused, as if he simply "runs the numbers" on the sum total consequences of every particular event to decide which children should live and which should die?

It is as if God looked down to consider whether Missy should live or die. "Let's see, if she lives, ten units of soul-making goodness will be produced. But if she dies *fifteen* units of soul-making goodness will be produced along with four units of soul-destroying badness. Since her death will produce more goodness on balance, Missy must die." Doesn't this sound rather grotesque?

Within ethics, there is a theory like this called *utilitarianism*. The core of utilitarianism is that the right ethical action in any given circumstance is that which produces the greatest amount of total good. While this might initially sound plausible as an ethical theory, it implies that no action is intrinsically wrong. Every action is to be judged on the total good it produces, and if the rape and murder of a child produces the most good, that is the right course of action. But surely this cannot be right: some acts are always wrong whatever their consequences!

To sum up the problem, greater goods theodicy seems to present God as the ultimate utilitarian. Just think, every moment of every day God is allowing some individuals to undergo the most unspeakable suffering because of his greater purposes. Some are being butchered, others tortured, and others are slowly wasting away, all for the sake of producing a quantum of good. As Mack bluntly puts it, "It all sounds like the end justifies the means, that to get what you want you will go to any length, even if it costs the lives of billions of people" (125). As staggering as the statistic of billions of sufferers may be, for Mack the problem ultimately is centered on God's use of one little girl: "And what is the value in a little girl being murdered by some twisted deviant?" (125).

I have already noted that *The Shack* takes the bold stance that God allows every event as part of his purposes (125, 176). This entails that there was some sort of plan behind Missy's death: God foreknew and planned her death for a reason. So does the book offer a response to the charge that greater goods theodicy turns God into a cold, heartless utilitarian? Interestingly, the book appears to avoid this problem not by explaining how God might have used Missy's death, but rather by denying that he uses people in this way! Thus, when Mack complains that he cannot imagine any outcome that would justify evil, Papa tersely replies: "We're not justifying it. We are redeeming it" (127). This is significant, for rather than affirm that she is working both to justify and redeem evil, Papa denies altogether any justification. But this sounds more like the Open view of providence than an appeal to greater goods. Nor is this an isolated inconsistency. When Mack asks whether Papa planned Missy's death for the good of Mack's spiritual growth, Papa responds with an abrupt rebuke: "That's not how I do things" (185). With this rebuke she seems to reject not only Mack's proposed explanation for why Missy died, but also the very notion that there could be any explanation. And despite the fact that everything that occurs is taking place according to God's plan (125), Sophia is emphatic that *Papa did not plan* that Missy would be killed, for Papa does not need evil to accomplish her good purposes (165). Finally, when Mack charges Papa with using evil to force people back to her (a form of utilitarianism), again Papa rejects the very suggestion (190).

The Charge of the Protest Atheist

We find ourselves facing a puzzle. To begin with, *The Shack* affirms God's providential control over evil for his purposes. Just as God allows the suffering of the oyster to create a beautiful pearl (177), so he allows the suffering of creation to achieve greater goods. But then the book refuses at every point any suggestion that God allowed Missy's suffering and death to achieve greater goods. How does one explain this inconsistency? Is it simply a loose end in the text? Given the centrality of the question of evil, that would seem to be a pretty significant loose end. Could it be instead that *The Shack* recognizes that while greater goods theodicy may be great in the abstract, it becomes problematic when applied to specific circumstances?

To answer this question, let's consider the problem of Missy's death more closely. The problem with Missy's murder emerges in striking fashion when Jesus offers words of comfort to Mack by assuring him that both he and Sarayu were with Missy through her ordeal. When Mack asks whether Missy knew of their presence, Jesus replies: "Not at first—the fear was overwhelming and she was in shock. It took hours to get up here from the campsite. But as Sarayu wrapped herself around her, Missy settled down" (173). And then with some final words of comfort, Jesus adds: "I can tell you there was not a moment that we were not with her. She knew my peace, you would have been proud of her. She was so brave!" (173). Although these words offer some comfort to Mack, there is also something disturbing about them. The problem is that Jesus is not describing the bravery of a child who endured a flu shot or even a root canal. Rather this is God describing a child who endured unspeakable violations culminating in her own murder. How could Jesus and Sarayu have passively stood by as the killer had his way with Missy?

The problem with greater goods theodicy becomes painfully evident in the documentary *Deliver Us from Evil*. This unforgettable film chronicles the Catholic Church's sexual abuse scandal by focusing upon the crimes of Father Oliver O'Grady, a priest who molested dozens of children over several decades (some as young as nine months old). The film surveys the destruction O'Grady wrought in a number of lives including that of Ann Jyono. O'Grady started raping Jyono when she was but five years old, often in her home just down the hall from her parents. And he continued to do it for *seven years*. Although she is now thirty-nine years old, Ann remains haunted by the unspeakable horrors endured by that five year old. Needless to say her parents' discovery of this terrible crime has destroyed them. Now her once devoutly Catholic father looks into the camera and, with his voice quavering and his daughter weeping beside him, spits out the words: "I made up my mind. There is no God. I do not believe in a God, alright? All these rules, everything, they're made up by man, you know?"

If you want a vivid demonstration of the problems with greater goods theodicy, just look to Bob Jyono. Can we imagine finding a "word of comfort" knowing that Jesus and Sarayu were with Ann during her seven years of rape? Would we even dare to propose to those touched by this evil some greater good to justify Ann's nightmare? Is it any surprise that Mr. Jyono, convinced that there could be no explanation from a loving God, has rejected his religious belief?

Here we find ourselves in the deep waters of protest atheism. While the protest atheist may believe there is no God, his view is distinctive because he resolves that even if there were a God he would not recognize that God as a moral protest to the suffering in the world. I saw a vivid example of protest atheism some years ago when the prominent physician Canadian Henry Morgentaler debated William Lane Craig on the existence of God. During the question and answer section one young man asked Morgentaler whether he would bow to God if it could be proved to him that God existed. Morgentaler, who had once survived a German concentration camp, responded with thinly veiled disdain that he would bow to no one, God included!

It may well be that the most influential articulation of protest atheism in all literature is found in Russian novelist Fyodor Dostoevsky's master work *The Brothers Karamazov.* At one point in this labyrinth story the young priest named Alyosha meets his atheistic brother Ivan at a restaurant. It is not long before the conversation shifts to matters of God and Ivan presents the heart of his objection to God in a number of heart-breaking accounts of the abuse of children. Perhaps the most agonizing is the case of a five-year-old girl who was mercilessly beaten by her heartless parents:

> They beat her, flogged her, kicked her, not knowing why themselves, until her whole body was nothing but bruises; finally they attained the height of finesse: in the freezing cold, they locked her all night in the outhouse, because she wouldn't ask to get up and go in the middle of the night (as if a five-year-old child sleeping its sound angelic sleep could have learned to ask by that age)— for that they smeared her face with her excrement and

made her eat the excrement, and it was her mother, her mother who made her![6]

As Ivan would no doubt say, an evil of this degree is far in excess of anything that could possibly be justified as the route to a greater good. (Could God not have derived enough good from the child's beating alone? Did she have to eat her excrement too?) When the full implications are weighed, it seems that appealing to theodicy to explain such evil is not a consolation but rather an insult. Ivan continues,

> Can you understand that a small creature, who cannot even comprehend what is being done to her, in a vile place, in the dark and the cold, beats herself on her strained little chest with her tiny fist and weeps with her anguished, gentle, meek tears for "dear God" to protect her—can you understand such nonsense, my friend and my brother, my godly and humble novice, can you understand why this nonsense is needed and created?[7]

Ivan objects fundamentally to the very notion of theodicy for its unforgiveable conclusion that the torture, rape, and murder of little girls could be justified by God's cosmic purposes. Ivan's rage is palpable as he concludes his seething indictment against Alyosha's God: "Who wants to know this damned good and evil at such a price? The whole world of knowledge is not worth the tears of that little child to 'dear God.' "[8]

---

6. Fyodor Dostoevsky, *The Brothers Karamazov,* trans. Richard Pevear and Larissa Volokhonsky (New York: Alfred A. Knopf, 1992), 241-2.

7. Dostoevsky, *The Brothers Karamazov,* 242.

8. Dostoevsky, *The Brothers Karamazov,* 242.

For a protest atheist like Ivan, *this* is the final objection to theodicy and ultimately to God. No possible good could justify the tears shed by this child beaten and locked in the latrine, or those that soaked Ann's pillow as she was raped, or those that spilled onto the floor of the shack as Missy was murdered. Every attempt to justify and redeem such evils with respect to some hypothesized greater good only adds the final insult.

Why Is God Silent?

Any person with a modicum of sensitivity to suffering must surely admit the emotive pull in the protest atheist's position. But is an atheistic world where evil happens for no purpose really preferable? As difficult as it may be to stomach greater goods theodicy when it is applied to specific cases, surely the alternative is far worse! On this point the protest atheist is like the person who indignantly informs her doctor that she would sooner face death than the hopeful prognosis that comes through a course of chemotherapy. The greater goods explanation for evil does not offer an easy answer, but in contrast to atheism it does offer hope.

So why does God not make clearer his reasons for allowing specific evils? The first reason, which is implied by the inadequacy of greater goods theodicy when applied to specific cases, is that this knowledge would not be particularly helpful to us. Just as Jesus knew that it would not be helpful to give Mack specific details concerning Missy's ordeal (173) so God knows that it would often not be helpful for us to have the details of why we suffer. This was Harold Kushner's experience when he faced the imminent death of his son: "The books I turned to were more concerned with defending God's honor, with logical proof that bad is really good and that evil is necessary to make this a good world, than they were with curing the bewilderment and the anguish of the parent of a dying child."[9] Thus while theodicy may have great value in the ivory tower of speculative discussion, it is of negligible value for those in the trenches of suffering.

C.S. Lewis provides an excellent illustration of the point. This author of *The Problem of Pain*, one of the twentieth century's most effective theodicies, found his own book cold comfort when he lost his wife to cancer. And so in order to come to terms with his anguish Lewis wrote a very different book, *A Grief Observed*, in which arguments recede into the shadows. In their place we find agonized personal reflections: "People get over these things. Come, I shan't do so badly. One is ashamed to listen to this voice but it seems for a little to be making out a good case. Then comes a sudden jab of red-hot memory and all this 'commonsense' vanishes like an ant in the mouth of a furnace."[10] But even if the arguments of theodicy are vaporized in the furnace of suffering we ought not conclude that they are illegitimate or valueless, but simply that their application is limited. So in the case of Mack, it may be that Papa's refusal to provide a specific explanation for Missy's death is less a matter of inconsistency than the wisdom of a father who withholds knowledge that would be of little value.

---

9. Harold S. Kushner, *When Bad Things Happen to Good People*, 4.
10. C. S. Lewis, *A Grief Observed* (New York: Bantam Books, 1976), 2.

I would suggest a second reason why God refuses to explain why Missy died: those reasons may be too complex for Mack to understand. As Papa explains:

> There are millions of reasons to allow pain and hurt and suffering rather than to eradicate them, but most of those reasons can only be understood within each person's story. I am not evil. You are the ones who embrace fear and pain and power and rights so readily in your relationships. But your choices are also not stronger than my purposes, and I will use every choice you make for the ultimate good and the most loving outcome. (125)

Let's think about the claim being made here. In order to understand all the reasons why God allows a particular evil in someone's life, we must understand each person's story fully. So for Mack to understand why God allowed Missy's death, he would have to know her full story. And this would require him to know his wife's story, those of his children, and of countless other lives that Missy impacted through her life and death.

Perhaps you have heard of the famous butterfly illustration of how all things are intimately interconnected. According to the illustration, a butterfly's fluttering wings today in China could create thunderstorms next week in California. If the fluttering of a butterfly's wing could lead to such large scale effects in the world, what impact might the death of a child have upon the world? There could literally be *millions* of reasons why God allowed Missy's death as the impact of that event fanned out over the globe affecting innumerable other situations, all working toward God's final intention to weave the suffering of this world into a magnificent tapestry. It may be that the best we can do is trust that God has his reasons of which we cannot yet conceive (222).

Some years ago American public television (PBS) used to produce a program starring painter Bob Ross called "The Joy of Painting." Ross's enduring popularity came from his conviction that anybody could paint coupled with his easy and soft-spoken instruction. One of the most memorable moments of the program would come when Ross would be in the midst of a beautiful painting—perhaps a lovely pastoral scene with lake, trees, and mountains—and then he would suddenly scar the canvas with an ugly stroke of paint. "Oh no, Bob!" his viewing audience would cry out. "What a terrible mistake!" But then Ross would calmly assure the viewers that in painting there are no mistakes but only "happy little accidents." And with that he would methodically begin to transform that garish mark into a beautiful, towering pine tree that accentuated the painting in a way the viewer could never have anticipated.

At times, theologians have referred to the fall of Adam and Eve as a "*felix culpa*" or "happy fall." The point was not that the fall was a good thing, but rather that through this terrible event, God brought something wonderful in the life and death of his Son. Our challenge is to follow Mack to begin viewing the most garish scars of creation through the eyes of faith. Perhaps then we can begin to see that God will ultimately redeem each terrible event within an emerging picture of beauty in which there will no longer be mourning, crying or pain, for the old order of things will have passed away (Revelation 21:4).

DIGGING DEEPER

(1) Given that theodicy is of negligible value for aiding those in the midst of suffering, just what is its value?

(2) The assumption of the free will argument is that free will requires the ability to choose evil. Does that mean that God is not free since he cannot sin? And what about the human beings redeemed in eternity? If we will no longer be able to sin, will we not be free?

(3) Do you find the thought that Jesus and the Holy Spirit accompanied Missy throughout her ordeal comforting or disturbing?

(4) Do you believe that *The Shack* maintains the balance between God anticipating and redeeming sinful events without actually causing those events?

(5) How do you respond to the idea that God used Missy's murder to achieve greater goods?

CHAPTER 6

Finding Hope in God's Pain

One of the most haunting depictions of evil is found in Elie Wiesel's harrowing autobiographical account of the Holocaust in the book *Night*. Among the litany of horrors recorded in the book, the most agonizing may be the occasion when a small boy was sentenced to death on the gallows while the other prisoners were forced to watch. As Wiesel recounts, the horror was compounded by the fact that the boy's light weight led to a slow and torturous death by strangulation:

> For more than half an hour he stayed there, struggling between life and death, dying in slow agony under our

eyes. And we had to look him full in the face. He was still alive when I passed in front of him. His tongue was still red; his lips were not yet glazed.

Behind me, I heard the same man asking:

"Where is God now?"

And I heard a voice within me answer him:

"Where is He? Here He is—He is hanging here on this gallows . . ."[1]

While some readers interpreted Wiesel's comment as marking a retreat to atheism, in fact he was alluding to the mysterious notion that God somehow suffers with his people. Could it be that the sovereign Lord of the universe is present in and with a child facing the most horrific death?

Wiesel makes the point clear in his memoirs when he turns to address the problem of the Holocaust in a haunting three page mediation titled "God's Suffering: A Commentary." The passage begins:

Here is what the Midrash tells us. When the Holy One, blessed be His name, comes to liberate the children of Israel from their exile, they will say to him: "Master of the Universe, it is You who dispersed us among the nations, driving us from Your abode, and now it is You who bring us back. Why is that?" And the Holy One, blessed be His name, will reply with this parable. One day a king drove his wife from his palace, and the next day he had her brought back. The queen, astonished,

---

1. Elie Wiesel, *Night* (New York: Bantam Books, 1982), 61–2.

asked him: "Why did you send me away yesterday only to bring me back today?" "Know this," replied the king, "that I followed you out of the palace, for I could not live in it alone." So the Holy One, blessed be His name, tells the children of Israel: "Having seen you leave my abode, I left it too, that I might return with you."[2]

Just as God offers Job no explanation for his suffering, so in this parable the king offers no explanation for why he sent his queen out of the palace. Even while evil remains a mystery, the parable assures us that the king was with his queen in the midst of her suffering. Similarly, God offers no clear and specific reasons why he has allowed his people to experience incredible suffering—but he does promise that he is present with them in the midst of it.

This perplexing parable of the king's self-imposed exile takes on a whole new level of meaning for the Christian who believes that God has accompanied his people into exile by literally becoming incarnate in their midst. God does not merely suffer and identify with us as God—in itself a profound and perplexing notion—but as a human being as well. By identifying with human suffering God stood in solidarity with all the suffering and pain of this world. Could it be that here, in the weakness of the cross, we find God's final triumph over evil?

---

2. Elie Wiesel, *All Rivers Run to the Sea* (New York: Alfred A. Knopf, 1995), 103.

Jesus Suffered with Us

On the long drive up to Wallowa Lake, Mack shared with his children the legend of the Indian princess of the Multnomah tribe. According to the story, a sickness broke out among the men of the tribe and then quickly began to claim one victim after another. As the situation grew desperate, the medicine man shared with the tribe how his father had foretold years before that such an illness would strike the tribe. Further his father had said that the disease could only be cured if a chief's daughter should willingly surrender her life by throwing herself off a high cliff. Although the tribal leaders determined that they could never request that kind of sacrifice, one princess volunteered herself by journeying to the cliffs in the dead of night and casting herself to her death so that the tribe might live. In a miraculous commemoration of her sacrifice, the waters of the Multnomah Falls began to spill over the cliff from that point, marking the princess's gift with a perpetual cascade of living water.

Mack had always enjoyed sharing this story with his children, for "It had all the elements of a true redemption story, not unlike the story of Jesus . . ." (29). But while Missy was usually fascinated by the story, this time she appeared strangely subdued. The reason, as Mack later discovered, was due to the troubling connection between the Multnomah prophecy and God's seemingly cruel demand that Jesus must die to save humanity. In response, Mack explained: "His daddy didn't *make* him die. Jesus chose to die because he and his daddy love you and me and everyone in the world. He saved us from our sickness, just like the princess" (31). And so it is with this central

Christian doctrine that it presents us simultaneously with the mystery of God submitting his own Son to a sacrificial death, and the most glorious truth that he did it so that we might become his children. As important as theodicy may be for the Christian pondering suffering in the world, it is here at the foot of the cross that one encounters the greatest and final response to the problem of evil.

What sort of hope is found in the cross? To begin with there is the hope of solidarity that is found in the knowledge that God identifies with us in our suffering. God hung on the gallows with that child just as the king ventured out into the marketplace after his queen. I suspect that only people who have experienced very great suffering can appreciate the profound implications of this claim. To take one example, in the year AD 177 a vicious persecution broke out in Lyons (in what is today southern France) in which Christians were subjected to the cruelest of tortures. One young woman named Blandina was tortured for days while a young man named Sanctus writhed in agony as burning hot brass plates were pressed into the most vulnerable portions of his body. In addition, the church lost its beloved aged Bishop Pothinus after he received a severe beating. What would the cross have meant to the suffering saints of Lyons?

The answer came with Ireaneaus, one of the greatest theologians of the early church and the appointed replacement for Bishop Pothinus. In light of his church's experience with suffering, Irenaeus understood the significance of claiming that Christ stands in solidarity with us. He knew that because Christ had suffered with us, we could view our sufferings as a means of identification with our Lord (1 Peter 4:13). Irenaeus developed the implications of this teaching even as he sought to refute a popular heresy of the time called Gnosticism. According to Gnosticism, God could not suffer and since Jesus was God he only pretended to suffer on the cross. Irenaeus' reply came directly out of the incredible suffering experienced by his own church:

> If he did not really suffer, it is no credit to him, since there was no passion. And where we are concerned, when we begin actually to suffer he will seem a deceiver as he exhorts us to get ourselves beaten and to turn the other cheek, if he did not first suffer in the same way himself. Just as he led his disciples astray too by exhorting us to put up with things he did not put up with. What is more, we will be greater than our teacher inasmuch as we suffer and bear things which our teacher neither suffered nor bore.[3]

Let it never be said that theology does not have an impact on real life! As Irenaeus observes, if Christ was merely playacting on the cross, then Blandina, Sanctus, and Pothinus would have nothing to learn from him; indeed, they would have become greater than their teacher! In the same way that seasoned soldiers would not accept the appointment of a sergeant who had never seen combat, so Christian saints could hardly appreciate a savior who had never known suffering! As such, it was critical that the Lyons saints know that Christ had stood in solidarity with Blandina,

---

3. Ireanaeus, "Against Heresies," in Richard A. Norris, trans. and ed., *The Christological Controversy* (Philadelphia: Fortress Press, 1980), 53.

Sanctus, and Pothinus, and that whatever else they might face in the valley of the shadow of death, he would carry them through.

Jesus the Great Physician . . . and So Much More

As profound as it is to think of Jesus Christ identifying with us in our sickness, we could never be satisfied with a savior who only suffered with us. A patient ultimately seeks a doctor not simply so he can express empathy but rather so that he can bring healing. And we seek a God who gives not just his tears but a steady hand that will dry our tears. As Mack observes, Christ came to heal us of our sickness. But precisely how does that healing come about?

As we saw in chapter five, Mack's understanding of God's love is hampered by the very different fates of Amber Ducette and Missy. How could God be all-loving if he left Missy to die? In response, Sophia gives Mack a lesson he shall never forget when she turns his questions (or rather his thinly veiled accusations) back on him. The climax of her cross-examination comes when she demands that Mack decide which of *his very own children* he will decide to damn and which he will allow to be saved. Though Mack refuses to countenance this unthinkable choice, his interrogator continues to press the question. Finally, with an increasing sense of desperation, he pleads, "Could I go instead? If you need someone to torture for eternity, I'll go in their place" (163).

Though Mack does not realize it, with that desperate plea, he has found himself in rarefied company indeed. Recall Moses, who pleaded with God to forgive the Israelites for their worship of the golden calf. If God would not forgive, then Moses opted to stand in solidarity with his people by requesting that his own name be blotted out of God's book of life (Exodus 32:32). Remember the apostle Paul, who was so anguished at the plight of the Israelites that he expressed his own willingness to be damned if only in this way Israel might be saved (Romans 9:3). In this formidable tradition, Mack too expresses the willingness to be damned out of love for his children. But while our first reaction to Moses and Paul might be admiration for their selflessness, from another perspective one could argue that their positions were not admirable at all. To illustrate, consider a groom who misses his own wedding reception because he decided to offer his banquet meal to a homeless man. We would not consider this man's actions commendable! On the contrary, we would consider him to have insulted his bride and wedding party. Couldn't one argue by the same token that Moses, Paul, and Mack have insulted their God and the hosts of heaven by opting for finite and fallible humans?

The charge is an intriguing one, and when one thinks about it, it does seem sensible. The only problem is that it is shown to be false by the very heart of God. Moses and Paul were not deviating from the proper norm but rather were expressing the inexplicable love of God in the mystery of the Son, who opted to leave his perfect communion with the Father to realize our salvation. What is more, it is the Father who surrendered this perfect communion by sending him! Amazingly, for Moses, Paul, and Mack to surrender themselves for the sake of a suffering people is but one way to express the beauty of what Jesus did for us. In opting to die in his children's place, Mack has inadvertently expressed the very heart of God.

But what is it that Jesus did for us? As we saw in chapter five, the reality of evil is deep and perplexing. Any account of how God is working against and through it will inevitably be partial. The core term is *atonement*, the process of at-one-ment by which sinful creatures are brought back into relationship with God. How can we understand this mystery? Here we must return to the concept of accommodation that was central in chapter two. The fact is that we may not be able to understand literally how God has acted through the cross to save us, but he has revealed to us a number of accommodating images to explain aspects of this mysterious act of love in terms accessible to us.

In concluding this section, we will consider a few of these images. To begin with, our sinful state is often compared to sickness and even death to clarify that people are truly dead in their sins (Ephesians 2:1; Colossians 2:13). Absolutely unable to save themselves, it is Jesus who comes as the Great Physician to heal us from our sickness (Mark 2:17; Luke 4:23) and indeed to resurrect us back to life in his Spirit. The New Testament offers other accommodating images as well. For instance, Christ's work is described as a reconciliation (*katallage*), an image that calls to mind the settling of debts in the marketplace. Thus, God the Father "was reconciling the world to himself in Christ, not counting people's sins against them" (2 Corinthians 5:19; cf. Romans 5:11). In addition, Paul describes Christ's work in terms of redemption (*apolutrosis*), a term that calls to mind a person's liberation from slavery: "All are justified freely by his grace through the redemption that came by Christ Jesus" (Romans 3:24). Again, salvation comes from the grace of the Father through Christ.

The images are varied: we were dead and Christ brought us back to life, we were sick and he healed us, in debt and he paid for us, in slavery and he liberated us. And so when Mack asks what the atonement accomplished, Papa replies matter-of-factly: "Nothing much. Just the substance of everything that love purposed from before the foundations of Creation" (191).

As I said, the New Testament provides a number of accommodating images in Scripture, but not all of them make it into *The Shack*. Notably absent is the image of atonement as salvation from the wrath of God. This is not surprising given *The Shack*'s downplaying of the sovereign side of God. But the challenge for us is to ask whether the result is a truncated image of atonement. We shall ask this question in two steps, first by confronting the wrath of God in Scripture, and then turning to consider that wrath within the cross.

The Wrathful God

Ask most anyone to give an example of the low point in church history and they will probably point to the Crusades . . . and for good reason. Crusaders in the first sack of Jerusalem in 1099 proudly wrote home of how the blood from the Muslim infidels ran in the streets up to their ankles. Raymond of Aguilers, a chaplain in the army, recounts: "In all the . . . streets and squares of the city, mounds of heads, hands and feet were to be seen."

He concluded, "What an apt punishment! The very place that endured for so long blasphemies against God was now masked in the blood of the blasphemers."[4] Such accounts prompt one to ask how anyone could have carried out such atrocities while thinking they had the blessing of God! And yet, even if we accept that Jesus laid down a new ethic for the church, holy war was a familiar part of Israel's history. Indeed, Israel was sent in to conquer Canaan through the destruction of entire societies, infants and the elderly included (Deuteronomy 20:16–17).

No doubt Christians familiar only with the comfortable suburban God that has taken up residence in many North American churches will find the Old Testament accounts of holy war absolutely incomprehensible. As a result, they may seek to beat a hasty retreat to the meek Jesus who provides a marked contrast to the violent and capricious Old Testament God of war. As Mack puts it, "I understand Jesus' love, but God is another story. I don't find them to be alike at all" (163).

But the reality is that "gentle Jesus" offers limited respite from divine violence. Indeed, when we turn to the book of Revelation we do not find a denunciation of the regional and ethnic violence in the Old Testament, but rather an elevation of it to a truly cosmic scale. Indeed, the images of violent judgment within this prophetic book dwarf the atrocities of the most violent battles of military history. In one unforgettable image, God's angel of judgment is described as gathering grapes from the earth and throwing them into the great winepress of his

---

4. Cited in Piers Paul Read, *The Templars* (Cambridge, MA: Da Capo Press, 2001), 83.

wrath where they are "trampled in the winepress outside the city, and blood flowed out of the press, rising as high as the horses' bridles for a distance of 1,600 stadia" (Revelation 14:19–20). The image calls to mind God exercising his wrath as he smashes rebellious sinners to a lifeless pulp under the divine heel, leading to a cascading river of blood both deep and wide! Nor is this promise of punishment a singular anomaly, for warnings against the impending judgments of hell pervade the New Testament (see for instance Matthew 25:41,46; Jude 7).

Few Christians are *glad* to find such stomach churning images in Scripture (and we would certainly have our worries about those who were glad). Still the fact remains that the violence is there, and somehow or other it must be addressed. But how? How does one reconcile the God of seething wrath with the image of a loving Jesus who embraced the prostitute and tax collector? Surely we can sympathize with Mack's puzzlement when he asks:

> "But what about your wrath? It seems to me that if you're going to pretend to be God Almighty, you need to be a lot angrier."
> "Do I now?"
> "That's what I'd think. Weren't you always running around killing people in the Bible?" (119)

Mack has raised a fair question. If anything the image of God in *The Shack* simply compounds the problem. If Papa really is so jolly, easy-going, and submissive, then why does she come across in Scripture as dangerously violent?

Indeed, after reading the accounts of Scripture, a person could be led to suspect that at some deep level God enjoys the violence. When Mack boldly inquires as to whether this is true of Papa, he is taken aback by her response: "He could see a deep sadness in her eyes. 'I am not what you think I am, Mackenzie. I don't need to punish people for sin. Sin is its own punishment, devouring you from the inside. It's not my purpose to punish it; it's my joy to cure it'" (119–120). Note the significance of Papa's response. Not only does she make clear that she does not enjoy punishing people in hell, but she adds that she does not actually punish people at all. Rather, God simply leaves rebel human beings to their own sinful wills to be punished by the consequences of their own choices.

This notion that God does not actively punish people in hell was popularized by C.S. Lewis who famously described the gates of hell as being locked from the inside, a phrase that suggested it was human will alone that kept people in hell. Unfortunately that claim does not appear particularly plausible given the prevalence of New Testament images that describe God actively casting human beings into the furnace or outer darkness of eternal punishment (Matthew 8:12; 13:42; 22:13; 25:30; Revelation 14:9–11; 20:15). Whatever else we might conclude about God, Scripture certainly seems to teach that he will exercise a fierce and wrathful judgment against those who are not found in Christ (Romans 8:1). It would seem that the wrath of God is not so easily avoided.

Did Jesus Save Us from God's Wrath?

In addition to all the other problems human beings face—dead in sin, sick, in debt, and enslaved, we now find the most disturbing fact of all: we are all under the holy wrath of God! But if those who are not found in Christ face God's wrath, then this suggests something truly remarkable about the atonement: namely that in his atoning death on the cross Jesus absorbed God's wrath. Could this also be an accommodating explanation of the mystery of atonement? The evidence for this imagery is found in two Greek words—*hilasterion* and *hilasmos*—which have often been translated as "sacrifice of atonement" or "atoning sacrifice":

> Romans 3:25: "God presented him as a sacrifice of atonement, through faith in his blood.

> 1 John 2:2: "He is the atoning sacrifice for our sins, and not only for ours but also for the sins of the whole world."

> 1 John 4:10: "This is love: not that we loved God, but that he loved us and sent his Son as an atoning sacrifice for our sins."

The meaning of the words "sacrifice of atonement" and "atoning sacrifice" includes the concept that upon the presentation of the sacrifice, God's wrath is satisfied, that is he is *propitiated*. To be propitiated simply means to have your wrath turned away or satisfied.

For instance, imagine that you become enraged after you discover that your car has been vandalized. Now imagine how your anger would dissipate if the teenager responsible were to come to your door, consumed by guilt, with a tearful apology and an offer to make full reparations. No doubt unless you have a heart of stone you would find your anger melting away with this act of reconciliation: in this way you would have been propitiated or satisfied. This image of atonement suggests that in a similar way God is outraged against our sin but that in the death of Christ his wrath against us is satisfied.

Even as we explain atonement as the satisfaction of God's wrath, we need to be careful to avoid the danger of pitting a wrathful Father against a compassionate Son. Although it may be natural to think that because God is wrathful he therefore cannot act out of love, Scripture will not allow it. Rather, it is the *Father* who has acted out of love to reconcile us to him (2 Corinthians 5:19) through the death of his Son (John 3:16; 1 John 4:10). It is the *Father* who sent the Son to propitiate his wrath against our sin.

Confused yet? Nobody said that understanding the atonement would be easy. Even if we cannot get the mechanics quite clear in our minds, we should strive to be faithful to the images revealed to us. And here the key point is that the atonement is an act of the Father's love. As John Calvin put it, "For it was not after we were reconciled to him through the blood of his Son that he began to love us. Rather, he has loved us before the world was created, that we also might be his sons along with his only-begotten Son."[5]

---

5. John Calvin, *Institutes of the Christian Religion*, vol. 1, ed. John T. McNeill, trans. Ford Lewis Battles (London: SCM Press, 1961), 506.

In place of the image of the Father visiting wrath upon the Son, *The Shack* depicts the Father as *suffering with* the Son! Thus when Mack incredulously asks Papa how she can sympathize with his experience of losing Missy, she sadly looked down at her hands. "His gaze followed hers and for the first time Mack noticed the scars in her wrists, like those he now assumed Jesus also had on his. She allowed him to tenderly touch the scars, outlines of a deep piercing, and he finally looked up again into her eyes. Tears were slowly making their way down her face" (95–96; see also 222). This theme of the Father's suffering is reiterated elsewhere in the book. Consider when Sophia asks Mack:

> "Haven't you seen the wounds on Papa too?"
> "I didn't understand them. How could he . . ."
> "For love. He chose the way of the cross where mercy triumphs over justice because of love." (164–165)

The claim that the Father was wounded on the cross, that he too was victim in the death of Christ, is startling and so requires a closer examination.

Some critics have charged these passages with modalism based on the claim that the Father bears the marks of crucifixion. However, the argument of the text is not that the Father was the Son on the cross, but rather that the Father suffered *with* the Son on the cross. If these passages are troubling, it is not because they suggest modalism, but rather because they replace the divine wrath with an unrestricted conception of divine suffering. However, the book is ambiguous about the extent to which Papa is open to suffer since she also makes claims that suggest she exists beyond suffering: "By nature I am completely unlimited, without bounds. I have always known fullness. I live in a state of perpetual satisfaction as my normal state of existence" (98; see also 97–98).

Charting the Limits of Salvation

When I was growing up, I came to believe that the pinnacle of evangelism is found in the fearless street preacher who stands boldly on the street corner proclaiming the gospel while thrusting little booklets on the Four Spiritual Laws to every passerby. To be saved by Christ meant that you had to recognize your sin, and accept Jesus into your heart. Today I have come to realize that things are not that simple, or if they are there is at least no consensus within the Christian community on it.

The question of the limits of salvation has long been debated among Christians. As such, it is not surprising that the discussion finds its way into *The Shack* as well. Consider the following conversation between Jesus and Mack:

"Those who love me come from every system that exists. They were Buddhists or Mormons, Baptists or Muslims."
"Does that mean," asked Mack, "that all roads will lead to you?"
"Not at all," smiled Jesus . . . "What it does mean is that I will travel any road to find you." (182)

This exchange has ignited a significant amount of debate. What precisely does it say about salvation, and is that message compatible with Christian conviction?

Some critics have charged *The Shack* with pluralism, namely the view that there are many ways to be saved, and Jesus is but one of them. While this is a popular view in our contemporary pluralistic culture, it is not compatible with Christian belief in the uniqueness of Christ (John 14:6; Acts 4:12). Fortunately, pluralism is not to be found in *The Shack*. As Jesus makes clear to Mack, if you are saved it means that Jesus found you!

The real question at issue concerns *how* salvation comes through Christ. The view with which I was raised said that people must know about Jesus and pray the sinner's prayer in order to be saved. This is a form of exclusivism according to which a person must hear the gospel in order to be saved by it (see Romans 10:8–15). While exclusivism has been the predominant position in the history of the church, there has always been a minority opinion known as *inclusivism*. According to this view a person can be saved by Christ without having heard the name of Christ. Most Christians are already inclusivists regarding the salvation of Old Testament believers, infants, and the severely retarded. So might it not be true also of some lost souls in far off lands who have never heard the gospel?

Does *The Shack* provide us with some insight into these questions? Early on in the book when Mack is talking with Missy about Jesus' death, she asks about the notion of God in the Multnomah Princess legend:

"Is the Great Spirit another name for God—you know, Jesus' papa?"

Mack smiled in the dark. Obviously, Nan's nightly prayers were having an effect. "I would suppose so. It's a good name for God because he is a *Spirit* and he is Great." (31)

Does Mack's answer support inclusivism? After all, it implies that Native Americans who had never heard the gospel still had some knowledge of God. While this is true, the text says nothing about whether that was a *saving* knowledge. In that regard, Mack's claim that the "Great Spirit" is the Christian God is no different from Paul's argument that the Unknown God at Mars Hill is the Christian God (Acts 17:23).

A similar ambiguity accompanies Jesus' earlier exchange with Mack. Consider again his words: "Those who love me come from every system that exists. They were Buddhists or Mormons, Baptists or Muslims" (182). This could mean that there are Buddhists, Mormons, and Muslims (even Baptists!) who will be saved by Christ, perhaps all of these (excepting the Baptists) without a prior knowledge of Christ. But note the ambiguity. Jesus does not say that they were saved as Buddhists, Mormons, and Muslims, but rather that they were once Buddhists, Mormons, and Muslims. In other words, this may express nothing more than God's intent to make disciples of all nations (Matthew 28:19), a confession that is fully compatible with exclusivism. It would seem that the book is not as concerned with delimiting the precise extent of the potential application of Christ's atonement as affirming that the atonement is the single means to reconciliation with God, an act rooted in God's love for all his children (163).

In closing, let's return to the evocative statement that even some Baptists will be saved by Christ. While one might take this to be a cheeky devaluation of the organized church, it strikes me rather as a very sober warning that we ought never think we have "arrived" simply because we identify ourselves as Christians. Paul commanded us to test ourselves to see whether we truly are in the faith (2 Corinthians 13:5). It is surely a good practice, for according to the parable of the sheep and the goats (Matthew 25:31–46) there may be many Baptists (and Lutherans, Catholics, and Pentecostals) who will boldly approach the throne as proud sheep, only to find themselves consigned to "the eternal fire prepared for the devil and his angels" (Matthew 25:41).

DIGGING DEEPER

(1) A key theme in *The Shack* is that God is especially fond of *everybody*, and thus that Christ died for all people (1 John 2:2). How can this be reconciled with texts that suggest Christ died only for the church (John 10:11; Acts 20:28; Ephesians 5:25)?

(2) Sophia challenges Mack's belief that God chooses some people for hell (162). But if God knows the future and thus creates some people knowing that they will choose hell, has he not indirectly chosen their destiny?

(3) What do you think of the notion that God's wrath was upon Christ? Do you prefer *The Shack*'s depiction of the Father as suffering *with* Christ?

(4) Do you believe that people can be saved by Christ without ever having heard the gospel? What biblical basis would there be for that view? Does it have particular dangers?

CHAPTER 7

WHEN ALL WILL
BE MADE NEW

I n 1990 NASA turned the cameras of the space probe Voyager 1 back around to photograph the planet that it had left thirteen years earlier. From this distance, far out on the edge of the solar system, the earth appeared to be a faint, blue dot, barely visible in a sea of stars and inky blackness. And yet those humble images that the Voyager craft sent back to earth were of great existential import, for no human being had ever seen the earth set against this truly cosmic backdrop. It may have been just a dot but it was *our* dot. As Carl Sagan observed, "Look again at that dot. That's here. That's home. That's us. On it everyone you love, everyone you know, everyone you ever heard of, every human being who ever was, lived out their lives."[1]

Billions of lives have come and gone on this humble orb, "every 'superstar,' every 'supreme leader,' every saint and sinner in the history of our species lived there—on a mote of dust suspended in a sunbeam."[2] Within this vast universe it is a barely noticeable mote of dust, and yet for us it is of inestimable significance, home of great cities, magnificent civilizations, mass extinctions, terrible wars, snow-capped peaks, deep forests, ice ages . . . and one beautiful child taken all too soon. As we long for the redemption of the many lives that populate this globe, is there room to hope as well for this pale blue dot?

On the Very Idea of Saving Creation

Sadly, the question has rarely been considered by many Christians who have learned a rather skewed vision of the afterlife according to which, as Christian rock pioneer Larry Norman sang, we're only visiting this planet. According to this pessimistic vision, creation is doomed only to destruction. In the meantime, we are stuck here waiting for the completion of a cosmic rescue operation. According to this popular notion, Jesus went to his Father's home to prepare a place for us in the great heavenly mansion (John 14:2–3), though in our individualism, the promise has morphed into a vast subdivision of mansions, one for each saint! And so when the time is right Jesus will come back for the church

---

1. Carl Sagan, *Pale Blue Dot: A Vision of the Human Future in Space* (New York: Random House, 1994), 6.
2. Carl Sagan, *Pale Blue Dot*, 6.

so that we will be "caught up together . . . in the clouds to meet the Lord in the air. And so we will be with the Lord forever" (1 Thessalonians 4:17). At that point the curtain is raised for the final fate of the world. As the redeemed saints watch from a safe distance, a grand symphony of destruction will then unfold: "The heavens will disappear with a roar; the elements will be destroyed by fire, and the earth and everything done in it will be laid bare" (2 Peter 3:10). Yah! Take that earth!! And with that, this pale bluish smudge will be wiped off the horizon forever.

Based on these assumptions, many Christians have been distinctly sour on creation, appropriating John's warning with aplomb: "Do not love the world or anything in the world" (1 John 2:15). On this view, human beings are the eternal apple of God's eye. As for creation, it's nothing more than the disposable apple box. With this negative view of creation, it is surely surprising to hear Jesus share with Mack his deep care for the world. The exchange is prompted when Mack expresses admiration for the beauty that lies all around him. In response Jesus wistfully observes: "Can you imagine this scene if the earth was not at war, striving so hard just to survive?" (144).

Could it be that there is in these words a hint that we can hope for something more for creation? Might love for this world (and indeed all creation) be not a mistaken apportioning of affection, but rather a reflection of God's love for his handiwork? As they continue their conversation, Jesus explains to Mack that his care indeed encompasses the entire cosmos. For too long, he explains, earth has been left to wander alone like a parentless child while human beings, who were chosen as its stewards, have instead set about plundering it.

These words are certainly a surprise for Mack who had long assumed the common view of creation as being like a condemned building awaiting the demolition crew. As yet this is a lot to digest in one sitting. As such, Mack tentatively seeks further clarification by asking whether Jesus is an ecologist. In response, Jesus provides an affectionate description of creation: "This blue-green ball in black space, filled with beauty even now, battered and abused and lovely" (144).

Jesus' love for creation is clear. Though battered and abused, it is still *his* creation, the one that he formed together with his own hands (John 1:3; 1 Corinthians 8:6; Colossians 1:16). And to think that the whole time Jesus was speaking with Mack, he was also upholding all 100 billion galaxies in existence (Colossians 1:17; Hebrews 1:3)! Is it any wonder that Jesus senses a certain ownership over creation? Indeed, he is downright possessive! As Abraham Kuyper once said, "There is not one square inch of the entire creation about which Jesus Christ does not cry out, 'This is mine! This belongs to me!' "[3] If this is his creation that he brought into being and that he sustains, then why wouldn't he want to save it all, our pale blue dot included (144)? Could it be that "for God so loved the world" encompasses not simply the inhabitants of the world, but indeed the very world itself?

---

3. Cited in Richard J. Mouw, *Uncommon Decency: Christian Civility in an Uncivil World* (Downers Grove, IL: InterVarsity Press, 1992), 147.

Redeeming the Shack

The shack is an old building in the Oregon wilderness that serves as a backdrop for Missy's death and Mack's encounter with God. But it is also a symbol for those places of private pain in which we bury our deepest sorrows. This private, therapeutic conception of the shack also applies to Sarayu's work in the garden which, as she explains, represents the chaos and beauty of Mack's soul (138). Presumably then, when Missy is buried in the garden it represents the inner healing that is brought to Mack and his anticipation of a reunion with his beloved daughter. From this perspective, the entire weekend represents a profound inner journal of spiritual healing and growth, not unlike Teresa of Avila's *The Interior Castle*.

However, *The Shack* is not simply about one individual's introspective journey. Even as the shack and the surrounding environs represent Mack's inner life, they also provide a very public glimpse of the healing that God is bringing to all creation. Let's return to that moment when Mack, having found the shack empty, is journeying back up the trail to the truck. Suddenly he is enveloped by a strange warm breeze. As he turns around in surprise, the wintery forest begins to transform miraculously before his eyes as the onset of spring begins to unfold in a matter of seconds. The snow quickly melts, revealing lush green growth while the large flakes of snow that were tumbling down to earth are now replaced by twirling flower blossoms. Within minutes winter's lock upon the land has been broken and spring has returned. (A reader of C.S. Lewis must surely find here some resonance with the liberation of Narnia from the wintry grip of the White Witch!)

But the biggest surprise is yet to come as Mack turns back around to behold the shack of horrors, for it appears to have been "replaced by a sturdy and beautifully constructed log cabin" that "was built out of hand-peeled full-length logs, every one scribed for a perfect fit" (81). Instead of that decaying, ramshackle hovel, Mack now sees a completely new cabin that would complement any trendy ski resort. But things are not quite what they seem. After Mack has spent some time in this beautiful new cabin, he walks into the front room and begins to wonder: "Could this even be the same place? He shuddered at the whisper of lurking dark thoughts and again locked them out" (89). And yet, as Mack surveys the room, his nagging suspicion is confirmed: it *is* the same shack: "Glancing around the corner into the living room, his eyes searched out the spot near the fireplace, but there was no stain marring the wood surface" (89). In other words, though the building looks different, the interior space still includes the spot near the fireplace where Missy's bloody dress had been found. Despite the radically different appearance, this homey log cabin is indeed the same shack!

The same theme of transformation applies to the landscape around the shack. Mack looks out on the surrounding scene where three-and-a-half years before, police dogs and FBI agents had scoured the area searching desperately for some sign of his daughter. While the scene is visibly different, it still is the same wilderness: "In the waning moments of twilight, Mack could make out the rocky shore of the lake, not overgrown as he remembered, but beautifully kept and picture perfect" (109). It is the same lake, but the rocky shore is no longer forbidding and chaotic; rather, order has been brought to this world. Although the surrounding forest, lake, and mountains have changed significantly, this is the same bucolic forest setting.

Not only is everything different here, but it is also more real: the scones are more delicious, the stars are brighter, the lake is more serene, the mountains are more majestic. When Mack enters the wild beauty of Sarayu's garden he is enveloped by smells "so strong he could almost taste them" (130). Not only is everything more real, but it is all the way it should be. There is true peace within creation. Indeed, creation in this form provides a marked contrast to the world to which Mack returns when he awakens from his weekend. He even reflects that after his return, "It was more likely he was back in the un-real world" (237). Here we see the promise that God will not only save creation but in doing so he will make it into something much greater, that which he had always purposed for it.

The incredible lesson then is that God is not simply working to save Mack, Missy, and even the Little Ladykiller. Along the way he also intends to save that humble ramshackle cabin, the Willamette Valley, Wallowa Lake, the town of Joseph, Multnomah Falls, and the rest of creation distorted by the fall. The extraordinary scope of the claim should stagger us even as it draws us to praise: that every action, every event, is stitched seamlessly together to bring God's purposes to bear within his creation.

Rediscovering the World's Hope

This vision may be appealing, but is there reason to think that God really does intend to heal all of creation? In fact a closer analysis of Scripture will confirm *The Shack*'s hopeful vision while exposing the familiar picture of an ethereal life in heaven as a gross truncation of the gospel.

The problems begin with the fact that Christian funerals rarely if ever refer to the hope of the resurrection, opting instead to speak almost exclusively about the soul being with Jesus. But where did this idea come from? The consistent hope of Scripture is that our mortal bodies will be resurrected as spiritual bodies (1 Corinthians 15:42–44; see also Isaiah 26:19; Daniel 12:2). What is more, since Jesus' resurrection body is the first fruits of the resurrection (1 Corinthians 15:20), we can learn about our future body by looking to his. At some points Jesus' resurrection body appears to be different: for instance, he was not immediately recognized by a number of those he encountered (Luke 24:31). However, two things are clear. First, it is the very same body that was crucified on Friday which was resurrected on Sunday. (Otherwise the tomb would not have been found empty!) This identity was confirmed when Jesus invited Thomas to examine the scars in Christ's hands and side (John 20:27)! And so, if Jesus receives the same body (albeit glorified) then so shall we. Second, his body was physical for he could be touched by people and even eat fish in their presence (Luke 24:39). In the same way, our glorified bodies also will be physical.

This raises an important question: where do very physical people go to spend eternity? Certainly not in an ethereal heaven where they would fall through the clouds! And with this we turn back to Scripture to discover that the fullest picture of the future comes in the promise of a new heaven and new earth: "Behold, I will create new heavens and a new earth. The former things will not be remembered, nor will they come to mind" (Isaiah 65:17; see also Isaiah 66:22, 2 Peter 3:13, and Revelation 21:1–3). But is this heaven and earth completely new or, as *The Shack* suggests, is it like our bodies the old world renewed? Although some have pointed to images of fire to conclude that this world's future is complete destruction (2 Peter 3:10–13), I would argue that the fire of this passage represents not destruction but rather purification (as it does in Isaiah 48:10).

In support of the understanding of creation as renewed, consider Paul's profound observation: "The creation waits in eager expectation for the sons of God to be revealed. For the creation was subjected to frustration, not by its own choice, but by the will of the one who subjected it, in hope that the creation itself will be liberated from its bondage to decay and brought into the glorious freedom of the children of God" (Romans 8:19–21). This passage teaches that creation fell along with the human fall; it was tragically dragged down by the very individuals commissioned to tend it. Yet there is hope, for God promises to liberate this creation in the same way that he is liberating his children. Thus, he will lead us all back into the fullness of life within him. As Papa says, "Well Mack, our final destiny is not the picture of Heaven that you have stuck in your head—you know, the image of pearly gates and streets of gold. Instead it's a new cleansing of this universe, so it will indeed look a lot like here" (177).

While *The Shack's* view of a renewed creation is quite admirable, it is a bit disappointing at one point since the harmony of creation is interrupted by the consumption of meat. Mack's first meal at the shack includes an unidentified roast bird (105), while his two breakfasts both include bacon (118, 219). Moreover he is encouraged to go fishing (88, 89); indeed, when Jesus and Mack are walking across the lake, Jesus excitedly chases a fish that he had been attempting to catch for weeks (175–176). The problem with these incidents is that God's desire to redeem creation appears to include animals. Note first that God's original intention was that human beings and all other animals would be vegetarian (Genesis 1:29–30); the eating of animals is thus a concession to our fallen world (Genesis 9:3). When God redeems the world, predation will cease and be replaced by peace among animals and persons alike (Isaiah 11:6–9, 65:25). It is unfortunate that *The Shack* didn't explore this theme in its vision of a renewed and restored creation.

That relatively minor quibble aside, *The Shack* draws us beyond our own suffering and sin to contemplate the place of our salvation within a universe that God desires to save as well. God promises not only to answer the groans and wipe the tears of his beloved human beings, but of his beloved pale blue dot as well (Colossians 1:19–20).

DIGGING DEEPER

(1) What do you think of the idea that Christians will not live in heaven when they did, but rather will inhabit a new heaven and a new earth?

(2) If we understand the renewal of creation as a form of salvation (Romans 8:19–21), then how can we work to save the world?

(3) What do you think is the place of animals in the new creation? Do you think it is possible to meet a beloved pet again?

THY KINGDOM COME

C an you get theology out of a novel? Contrary to the skeptical sentiments of the critic we met in the Introduction, it seems that you can. Indeed, our conversations over seven chapters have demonstrated that *The Shack* is brimming with fascinating theological questions and concepts. There is nothing so profound as the concept of God, and few things as shocking as the notion that the creator of all things would stoop to our level and reveal himself to us in a most personal and intimate way. This concept of divine accommodation is beautifully captured in *The Shack* as Papa comes down to Mack's level to meet him in his deepest pain with the healing embrace of a mother. And this matronly embrace is an invitation to experience the equally incredible reality of God as a loving community of three persons, a truth that too often has been relegated to the periphery of church life. Of course the novel's depiction of God is not perfect—for instance, it appears to underemphasize biblical conceptions of sovereignty and wrath—but then I would challenge the critic to light a candle in the darkness by offering his or her own narrative depiction of the triune reality. As you'll see, it isn't easy! Perhaps the most we can hope for is to attain glimpses of the beauty, harmony, and unconditional love at the heart of God. *The Shack* provides some fascinating glimpses indeed.

As profound as the questions raised by the concept of God are, they become even more bewildering when they meet the incredible suffering that so often grips this world. How do we bring together the loving God revealed in *The Shack* with the murder of an innocent young child? As we saw, it is at this point that various theoretical attempts to reconcile God to evil, so appealing in the abstract, become shocking when applied to the suffering of specific lives. The unresolved tension at the heart of the book is visible in the dissatisfaction of some readers who have complained (to me) that Missy is not miraculously brought back to life. Why is it that Missy, like Job's children, must remain dead? Why is it that Mack is denied a real embrace, forced instead to glimpse his beloved daughter through a veil? Here we are challenged to move beyond the limits of theodicy to embrace the discipline of patient and prayerful hope. Perhaps the final lesson of *The Shack* is that we should remain discontent with this world, not because we are destined to leave it, but because we long to experience God's final healing touch when his kingdom comes in power. Even in the midst of unresolved pain we are challenged to embrace the hope that Jesus shares with Mack: "For now most of what exists in the universe will only be seen and enjoyed by me, like special canvasses in the back of an artist's studio, but one day . . ." (144).